SKETCH

12.05.00

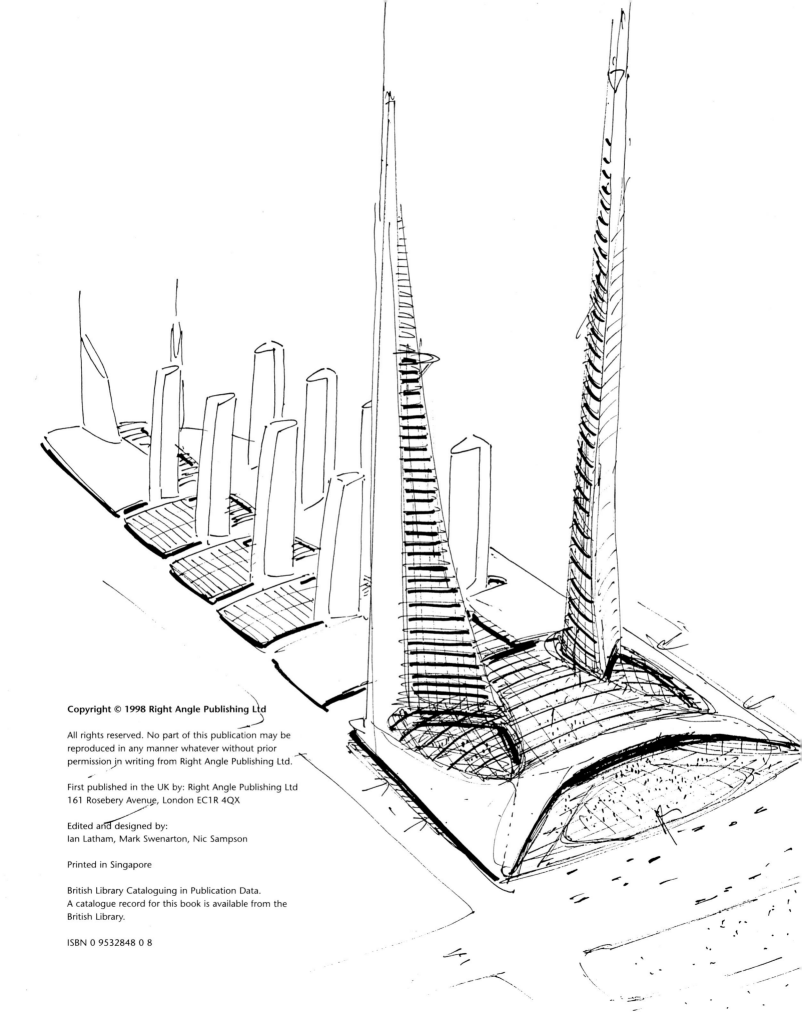

First published in the UK by: Right Angle Publishing Ltd
161 Rosebery Avenue, London EC1R 4QX

Edited and designed by:
Ian Latham, Mark Swenarton, Nic Sampson

Printed in Singapore

British Library Cataloguing in Publication Data.
A catalogue record for this book is available from the
British Library.

ISBN 0 9532848 0 8

SKETCHBOOK
12.05.98

RIGHTANGLE
PUBLISHING

Terry Farrell & Partners
with essays by Robert Maxwell and Terry Farrell

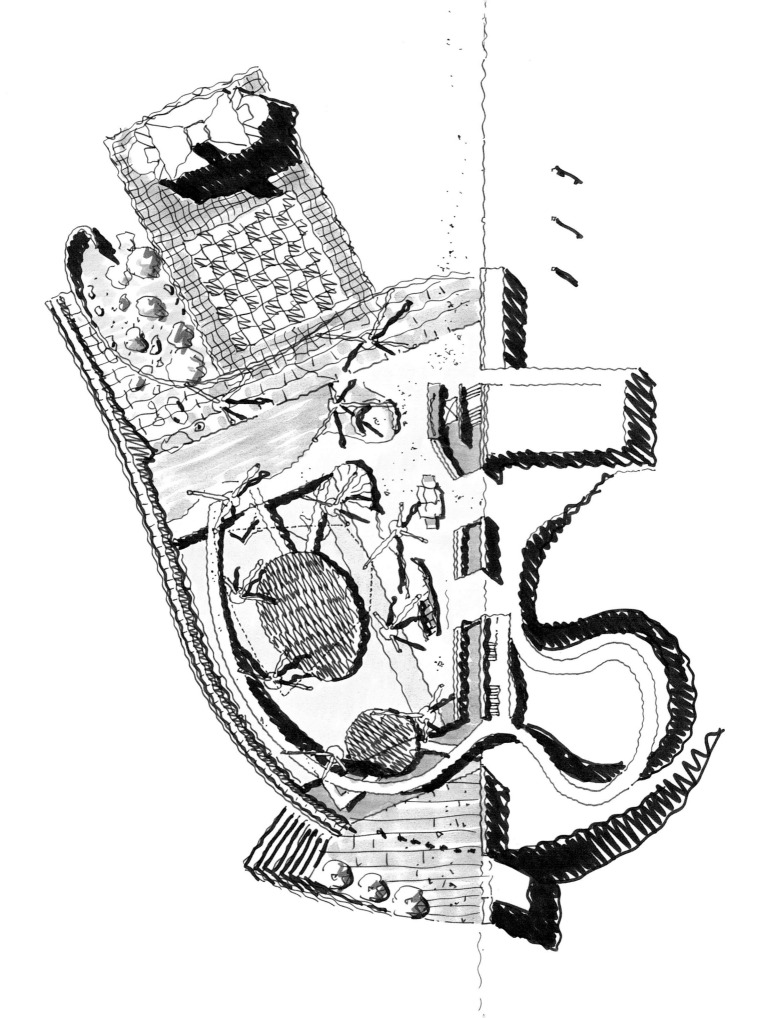

Cities in the making

Robert Maxwell

Terry Farrell began his career as a partner in the up-and-coming young practice of Terry Farrell and Nicholas Grimshaw, and I remember the surprise we felt when Richard Llewelyn-Davies hired them as whiz-kids to run a joint studio at the then very scientistic Bartlett School, where I was a teacher. That was in the mid-60s. Was Richard going to promote good design, as opposed to the prevalent fashion for programme analysis and design theory? One unexpected result was that they did a little building for University College London that was pretty ordinary, but distinguished by one cylindrical free-standing column, Corbusian but purple. The colour purple: could that have been a presage of a colourful future?

Then of course they split. Each became famous, and part of that fame was the contrast between their work. Not unlike the way that British jazz was illuminated when Ken Colyer and Chris Barber split the Dixieland scene in the mid-50s, one to pursue improvisational chaos, the other to promote cool and orderly arrangements. Grimshaw was henceforth seen as a high-tech boffin, Farrell as a PoMo terror. In Britain, this meant that their audience split too; one was orthodox, the other anathema inversely according to one's own preference. The fact was, they both developed very successful practices, and in Farrell's case, went global, with a large office in Hong Kong as well as London.

Today, Terry Farrell is one of the most exceptional architects practising in Britain and one of the handful of British architects who are personally successful at a global scale. His work has an amazing versatility, encompassing technologically advanced solutions along with environmentally sensitive schemes. Unlike some of his contemporaries, he does not expect form to emerge automatically from a structural or managerial analysis of the programme, but has no hesitation, after completing the analytical stage, in imposing an imaginative idea, a unifying theme, which ensures that the result has a clear intention. The building at the Peak, in Hong Kong, for example, has a distinctly Chinese silhouette that will look familiar to the locals but, seen

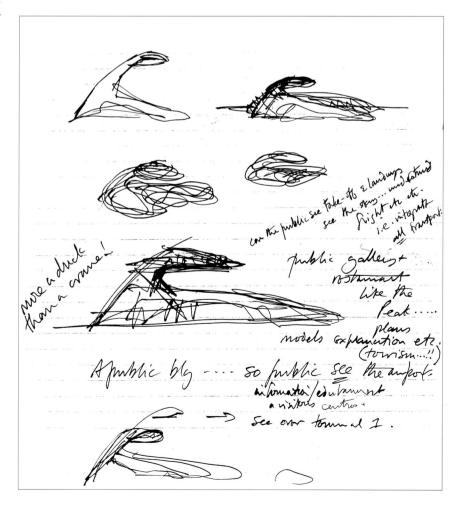

close to, it is free from facadism and appears as just a modern building. One could say that the work contains a semantic dimension, that it strives to produce meaning. At the same time it is imbued with a sense of reality and of what is economically feasible, so that it is immediately practicable and realisable.

Where his work has the most to offer, in my view, is through his sensitivity to context, and his corresponding ability to design buildings that are robust in their self-assurance yet fit into an existing environment and enhance it. This is particularly important for the future of cities. It is not always appreciated that cities are not produced by unitary systems of design, by the imposition of abstract 'zones' or transportation diagrams, but by the juxtaposition of buildings of varying and distinct character. This is how great cities have arisen and this is how they are recognised.

In my view, urban design is distinct from architectural design and in practice only emerges when architects know how to collaborate with city structure. Too often the large development resulting from a single financing initiative fails to integrate into the city but stands out as an over-designed enclave. The ability to exercise a fine judgement between the demands of continuity and the demands of novelty is a skill that few possess, and Farrell undoubtedly does.

He has demonstrated this ability in the series of masterplans that he has devised for large urban sites. Rather than seize on the opportunity to impose an aesthetic or systematic unity over the whole area, his approach has been to break the site down into plots, responding to the urban topography, orientation and the street pattern, with each plot capable of sustaining one building and the combination of buildings defining a distinct urban space – and the contributions by different hands projecting a visible variety. It is to be hoped that we will have the opportunity to see this eminently sane approach fully implemented before long.

As an architect of the single building, Farrell seems to search for the key factors that are unique to its programme, that will allow it to express its peculiar role as representative of an institution and so to take form as a building with its own distinctive character. Then it will contribute that character to its position in the city. It is not just a question of fitting in, of borrowing aspects from adjoining buildings in order to minimise the shock and harmonise the whole. Some shock is essential. This approach gives him a very special place as an architect with an understanding of urban structure, who is able to engage therefore in developments that result in urban design. It is in this sense that his vision of architecture embraces the goal of urban design.

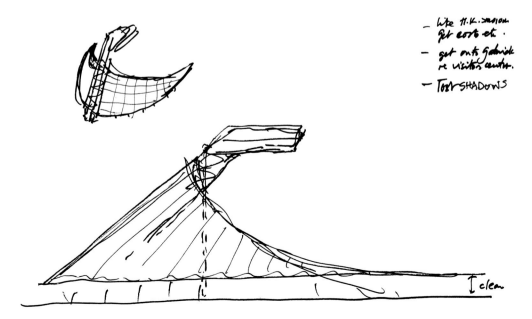

Whistling the tune: an inclusive view of architecture

Terry Farrell

I love what the eyes can see. The visual world, with its colours, forms and movement, is central to our experience and understanding of life. Buildings, towns and cities – our species habitat – are the most powerful and moving elements of our existence, as powerful as religion, music, art, or politics. But cities are and always have been more than these – permanent, public and shared in both expression and achievement. Architecture and urbanism, I have no doubt, are our greatest achievements.

My own work is driven by the desire to contribute to and celebrate all that is full of wonder and moving about this field. I subscribe to Keats' advice to Shelley: 'be more of an artist and "load every rift" of your subject with ore'. The liking of 'less' is based on a lie – it can only be held by those who already have 'more'. I do not believe that elitism and a taste for the minimal are the true marks of either the creator or the consumer of life's great visual pleasures. Maximalism is normal; eventually minimalism will be seen for what it is – a fetish, a self-deprivation or a quick fix delivering a momentary high.

I see place-making and artefact-making as the two core creative activities in architecture and urbanism. The former, concerned with space and identity, is the more profoundly important: enclosure, holding us all, creating a man-made world, making an identity, defining a position on the earth, an address –

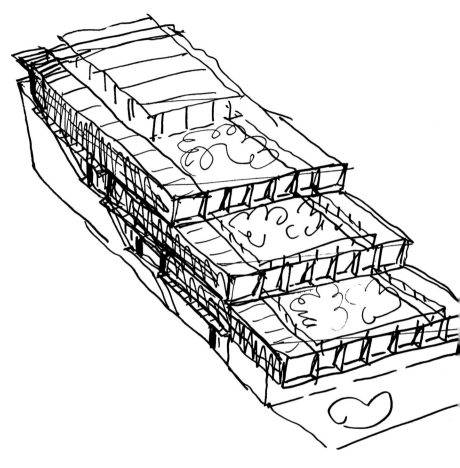

it's here, this is uniquely it. In contrast creating artefacts is much, although not solely, to do with construction. Construction is deeply gratifying when done well but it is not just a rational response to gravity and materials. Creating artefacts is much to do with deep psychological responses to shapes, colours and textures. At the most sublime the arrangements of these elements are phenomena that cannot be readily explained. The impulse to read and savour, commune and communicate, through shapes and colours is deep-seated and unites us through the experience of architecture.

To a large extent the story of art and architecture in the twentieth century has been one of the in-crowd versus the rest. The in-crowd, the modish or its corruption the 'modern', rely on groupiness. They belong to manifesto groups or fashion worlds from which they derive mutual support. Forward-looking is a cult – to be modish drives one not just to be ahead today but also to have answers for tomorrow (as in high tech – just how far ahead can you get?). But there is a basic need in art to express human experience as it is, not as it might or should be. For example, I find the Dadaists and Surrealists fascinating simply because they explored the darker side of humanity that exists in primitive as well as modern man. Similarly today's street art and street architecture give expression to decay, entropy,

chance and chaos – the complete antithesis of the 'we've got all the answers… tomorrow's world will be all white and silver' point of view. The resolution of these tensions in this most social of arts is best achieved by architects who are outside the mould, who cut across and change and diversify – and whose art as a result is more balanced and harmonious. In an ever-converging global world, independent divergent creativity is both rare and valuable.

I am fascinated by the conflict in today's world between the need for broad-based harmony and narrow specialisation. Cooperation across the globe is needed for a whole host of reasons – ecological, health, educational etc. But a global culture also means that, to make oneself seen and heard, an artist can feel driven to the extreme: the architect who builds only in white metal, or only in geometric raw concrete, focusses primarily on the headlines and winning awards from his peers. But this is the world of glossy magazines, art photos, brand imaging and taste experts, 'in the trade' not 'of the art'. I frequently recall Robert Venturi's inspirational writing some 30 years ago in Complexity and Contradiction in Architecture:

'Architects can no longer afford to be intimidated by the puritanically moral language of orthodox Modern architecture. I like elements which are hybrid rather than 'pure'; compromising rather

than 'clean', distorted rather than 'straightforward', ambiguous rather than 'articulated', perverse as well as impersonal, boring as well as 'interesting', conventional rather than 'designed', accommodating rather than excluding, redundant rather than simple, vestigial as well as innovating, inconsistent and equivocal rather than direct and clear'.

This view is threatening to the star system. Our market-driven world can force the able architect to almost caricature his own work in order to hold his niche. But a more humanist architecture must be much less self-obsessed and tramlined. The inspiration for creativity is the ability to make connections and this includes cities full of people, not a make-believe, self-deluding world of self-admiring architects and their supporters. Once, when asked by his father how he was getting on in Prague, Mozart said that he was doing very well indeed and 'even the errand boys are whistling my tunes'. If it's good enough for Mozart….

The most astonishing thing about postmodernism is how it has changed the world. This has been a bitter pill for those who still do not acknowledge its effects on our life but have nonetheless absorbed them and moved on enriched. But now we are all like Mozart's errand boys, whistling the tune – it's a postmodern world where urbanism is not anti-city and where history and context are part of every

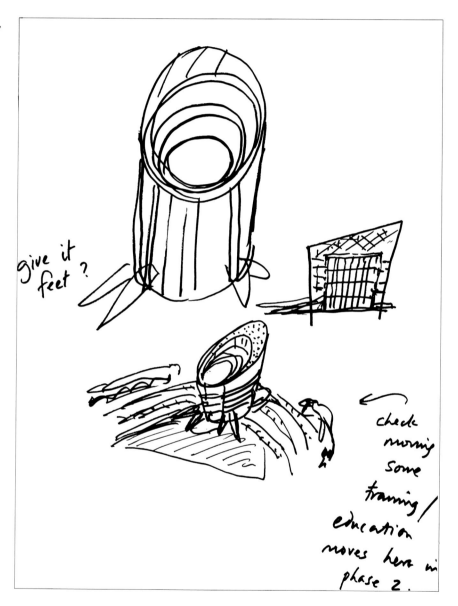

10

For Doug. re S'bury (< NB) (MJ) Pearson. Good Fri.!

What doesn't work is the effect of the roof appearing to have two big legs or props. These legs need to be done so that they do not seem to be columns/loadbearing.

One issue is that if you look at bldg. from low down (ground level.) the props look different. What can easily happen is that the glass skin reflects sky & the props are subsumed into the cladding.

In other words if the glass substantively builds around enveloping the prop then the prop is "there" but modified & reduced in significance. This makes them a critical difference between

glass — prop

The props as trim and the large curved trim elements on the roof which are outside & on top of the glass as fascia trims

(F)

---

architect's vocabulary.

Consistent with a wider, inclusive view of architecture is the conviction that urbanism is the key issue. The city is an uncontrolled manifestation; each city has its own brand of chaos theory. This is why it is so truthfully an expression of our condition and why cities are so exhilarating and so important an art form – the ultimate art installation. The best architecture grows from context and for the great majority of buildings this means the man-made context of urban life.

I have often thought that buildings could be put on a Freudian couch and analysed, for in them is exposed the architect's psyche. Repressions, phobias and pleasures and indulgences are all there to see. Some buildings are clean and tidy, with no clear entrances or orifices; others expose their private parts or inner plumbing to the outside. I believe these things are much more revealing and important than mere stylistic differences.

In a similar way cities tell us about a whole society – its attitude to and experience of power, the values it places on culture and on nature. Cities prove the invalidity of a 'pure' view of architecture. Some of the most visually arresting buildings and cities are unintentioned or were built by non-professionals or collectively. Cities are the best evidence yet for believing in our species and in its ability to prevail.

Learning through drawing

Nic Sampson

This is a book of drawings. It includes many sketches as well as photographs of models, collages and other graphic devices made by the staff of Terry Farrell & Partners over the last two years.

A successful drawing is a fusion of ideas that establishes its authority in an artistic as well as a constructional sense. But it should also be an indulgence – an opportunity to begin a journey without necessarily knowing the destination. 'Loose drawing' can help to define the architect's brief and encourage lateral thought. In some instances there may be a distinct advantage in not knowing quite where you are going!

Yet for the most part what many architects regard as a good drawing is probably not what the engineer or contractor would consider useful. Of all those involved in the building process, the architect is perhaps alone in believing that the drawing has some value over and above its literal role as a means to construction. In some ways the character of the drawing can anticipate or establish the demeanour of the completed building.

At Terry Farrell & Partners great importance is attached to the exploration of ideas and to this end considerable responsibility is vested in the drawing. It is a time-consuming and very demanding process where the author of the drawing has the responsibility of locking it into the greater thought-pattern

that shapes a project. Embedded within the work has to be a strong sense of 'achievability' at whichever level it's going to be read – artistic or realistic. Nothing is left to chance and the drawing is king.

Every significant 'move' on a project is modelled in the workshop, sometimes time and time again. Underpinning this is a recognition of the limitations of the brain in dealing with complex three-dimensional issues. Many architects won't admit to this, yet for Farrell it's not an issue, just part of the process 'sketch > model > refine > define'.

The idea for this collection of drawings came from the feeling that the large number of interesting projects currently in the office should be captured in some way. We wanted to bring to the fore early sketch ideas that often become obscured or superseded by the ultimate direction of a project. We also wanted to capture a point in time – what the office is doing now – to exhibit its talent and show the importance of creative exploration.

What are the themes running through the work? Urban design and a preoccupation with the complexities associated with the urban condition have long been a fascination for Terry Farrell. Most of the recent projects are not large interventions in the heart of London of the sort for which the office became renowned in the 80s. Nonetheless they retain similar interests – the urban preoccupation

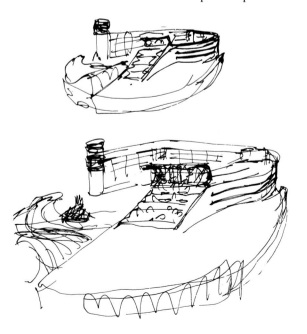

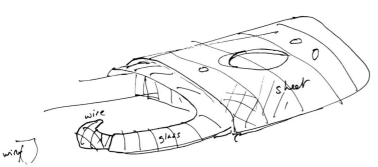

with the 'big move', synthesised with the inevitable collage thrown up by the city context.

Many of the projects in the book exhibit this 'big move' – a clear and singular architectural device that binds a scheme together. Some schemes, such as the Samsung headquarters in west London, remain as the big singular move. In others the move is a catalyst – like a coat-hanger – to give shape to a series of constituent components that find their own individual expression. This is the case with projects like the Centre for Life in Newcastle, a collection of city centre buildings for the next millennium, and the Blue Circle cement works, a little bit of 'town' in the Garden of England.

This approach however is not appropriate for every project. With the York city centre scheme, for instance, what is surprising is the degree of apparent restraint manifest in the sketches – yet architecturally it is one of the most challenging projects in the office. Some of the images are remarkable, simply for their unabashed attempt to explore a contemporary rhythm among some of the most historically distinctive buildings in England. In sharp contrast is the Northumberland Cross, a singular icon growing out of a defensive mott – a motif found incidentally in the centre of York. This is a project intended to celebrate the millennium and, like many late-twentieth century devices, demands

human interaction for best results! The images are strong and immediate yet also evoke something of the spirit and mystery of pre-Christianity.

The optimism of the work in the Far East is evident in the Integrated Transportation Centre in Seoul, based on the image of a bird first drawn by Terry Farrell on a restaurant napkin. An interesting feature of this project is the method developed by the team to expedite the translation from model – the only medium initially able to capture the silky three-dimensionality of the building – to the precision of the working drawing. Each model was sliced into countless sections, like brain scans, to reveal the sectional characteristics of the complex compound curves. These sections were then scanned into the computer before being remapped digitally. This technique was also used on the Centre for Life.

Perhaps the most idiosyncratic project is the Dean Centre in Edinburgh. What initially appears to be fairly unassuming is in fact a rich collaboration between architect and artist – Farrell and Sir Eduardo Paolozzi – where in true dialectical fashion the drawings produced by the office began to resemble the sculptures of the artist.

A sea-change is underway in the office. We hope that this selection, taken from the literally thousands of images being produced and developed, will reveal something about the richness of this process.

National Aquarium London

The National Aquarium is conceived as a 'core sample' of the world's habitat, with the earth, the waters and vegetation upon it and the air and clouds above, all in microcosm. The base is like geological strata – rocks and naturally-found metals are expressed in layers with fissures. Just as deformities in the earth's plates form mountains and seas, so the building breaks apart to create land and water forms. The cloud-like roof reacts to temper the climate below, adjusting to provide natural ventilation as needed. In summer the roof collects solar energy and moderates the sunlight while in winter transparent blankets of insulation reduce heat loss.

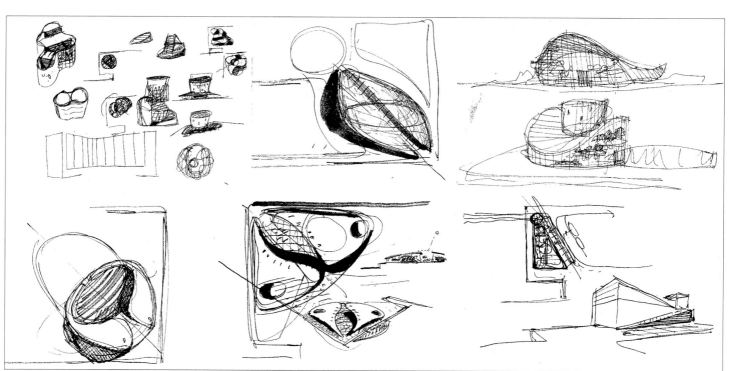

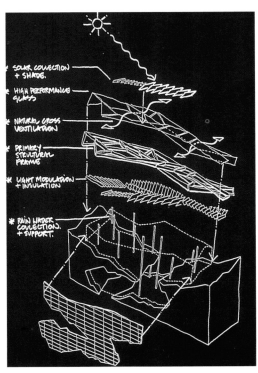

SOLAR COLLECTION + SHADE.

HIGH PERFORMANCE GLASS

NATURAL CROSS VENTILATION

PRIMARY STRUCTURAL FRAME

LIGHT MODULATION + INSULATION

RAIN WATER COLLECTION. + SUPPORT.

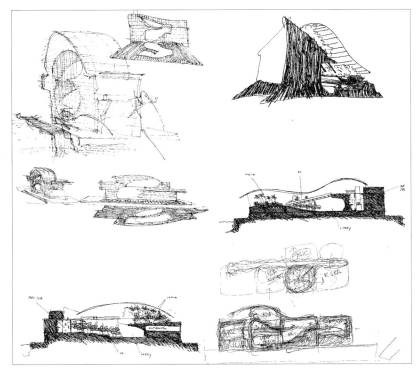

The National Aquarium building is arranged in four parts, each reflecting four world habitats. The central portion contains the UK freshwater display at the lower level, with the India display at the top. The UK exhibits spill out to the entrance area and coach and car arrival, introducing this primary exhibit to the visitor from the outset. The blank ends, clearly evident on the north and south sides, contain the tropical and sub-tropical areas of the Red Sea and South Pacific.

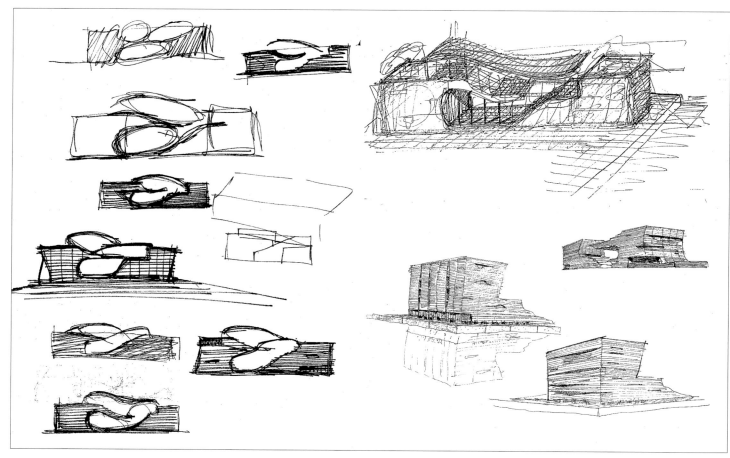

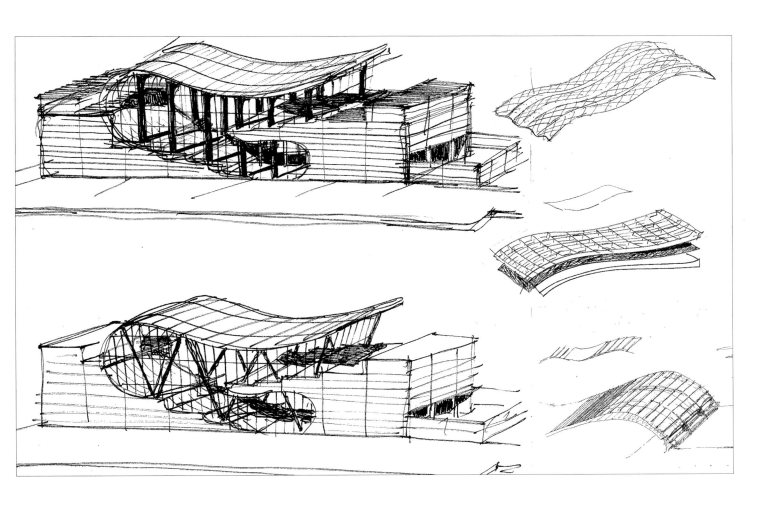

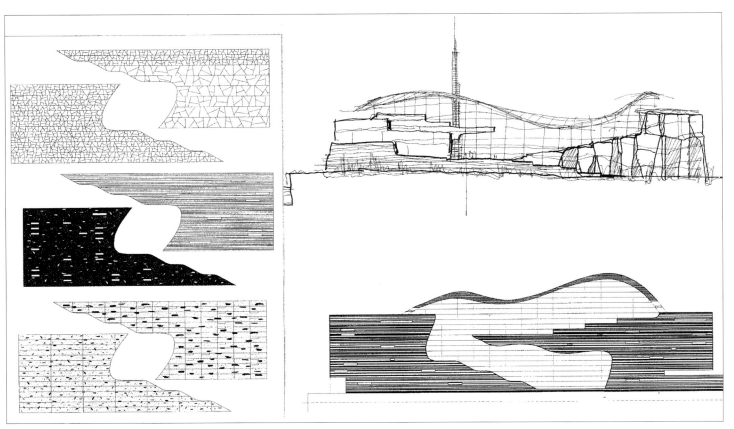

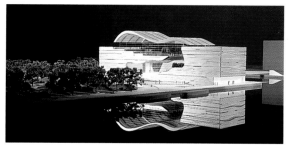

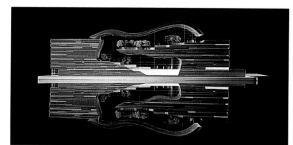

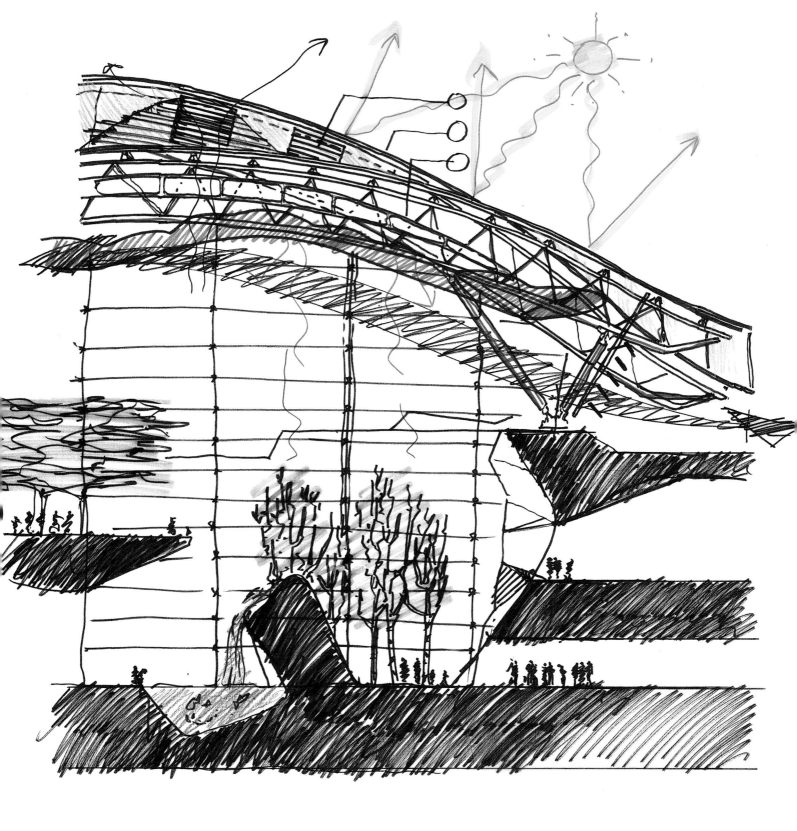

The National Aquarium building is conceived in terms of sustainability and conservation. The east-west orientation of the glazed areas allows cross ventilation in summer, with stratification of the air from the cooler UK exhibits to the warmer Ganges exhibits above. The two internal exhibitions of the South Pacific and the Red Sea act as thermal buffers against respectively the extremes of heat gain from the south in the summer and heat loss from the north in winter. The solid masonry walls help balance the temperature by forming natural heat sinks. Continuous monitoring will ensure that air and water heat retrieval and heat balancing integrate with the energy programme.

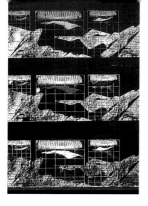

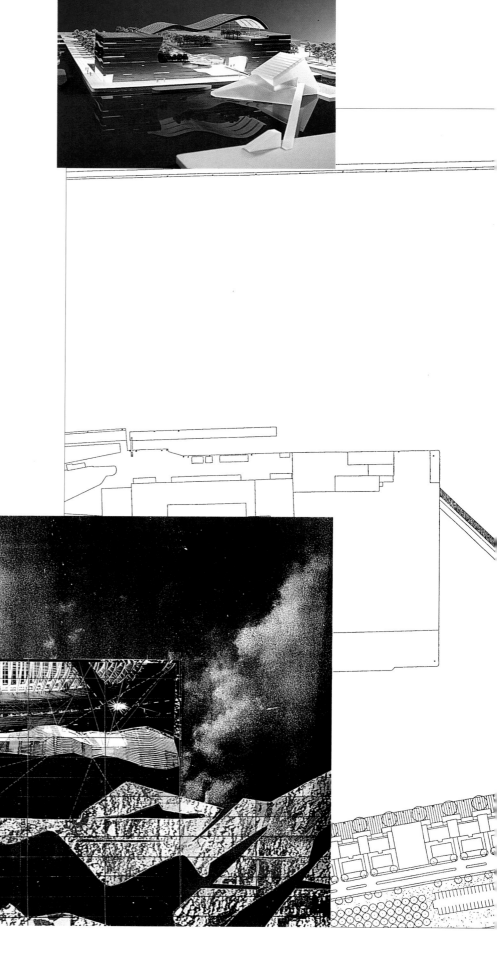

The National Aquarium is located on the edge of the Victoria Dock in east London. The building is placed at the extreme end of the site, a long thin strip sited on a peninsula, with deep water on the north, south and west. On the east (entrance) side the UK exhibit spills out into ponds and water courses which are crossed by the entrance paths and bridges, so that the building seems like an island from all viewpoints.

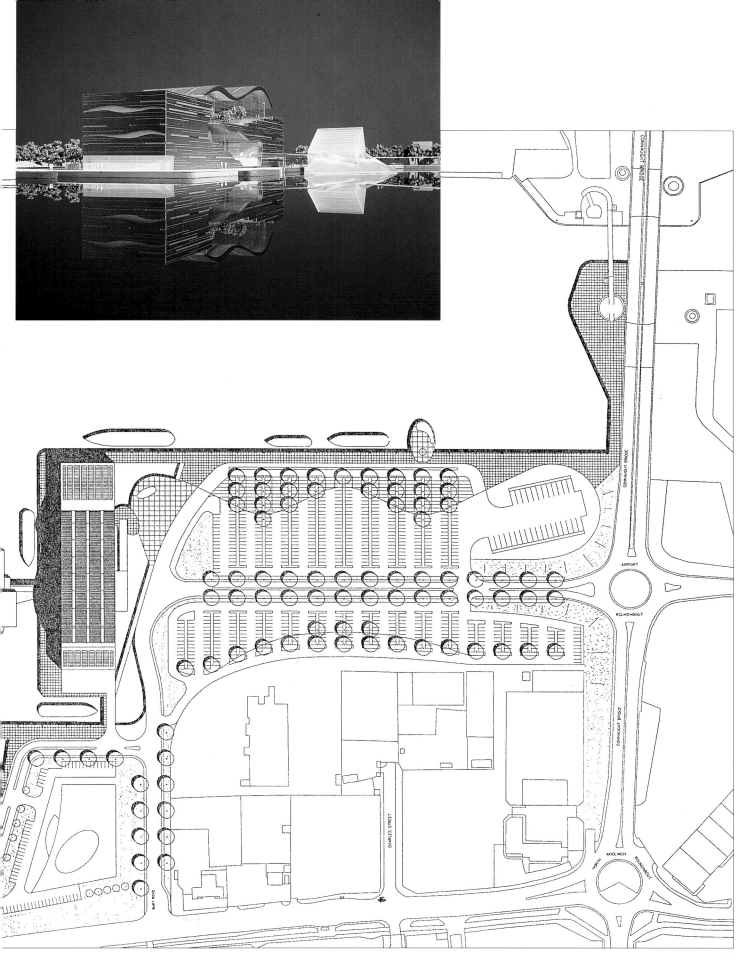

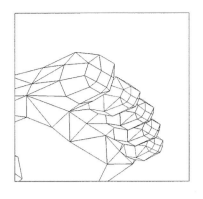
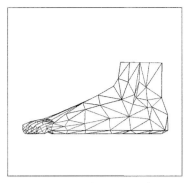
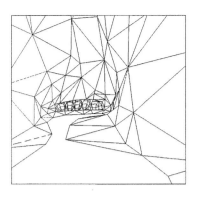
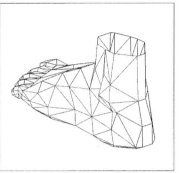
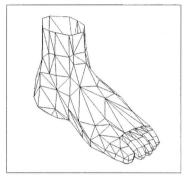
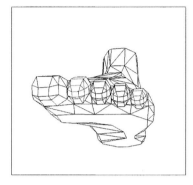

Dean Centre Edinburgh

The Dean Centre was originally designed as an orphanage by Thomas Hamilton in 1832. The grade-A listed building is now being converted for the National Galleries of Scotland as an art gallery to display the works of Scottish-born sculptor Sir Eduardo Paolozzi and to house the Dada and Surrealist collections of Roland Penrose and Gabrielle Keillor. Upper level galleries will also be used for temporary exhibitions.

One of the main issues was the setting of the Dean Centre in relation to the existing Gallery of Modern Art. The appropriately modest masterplan brings the two buildings together and encourages visitor flow. Other artists have been involved in the landscape design, for example the landform sculpture by Charles Jencks. The result is a single arts campus which engages with the riverside walks along the Water of Leith and the pedestrian routes leading into the centre of Edinburgh.

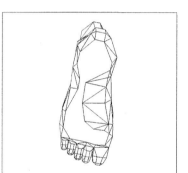
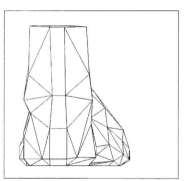

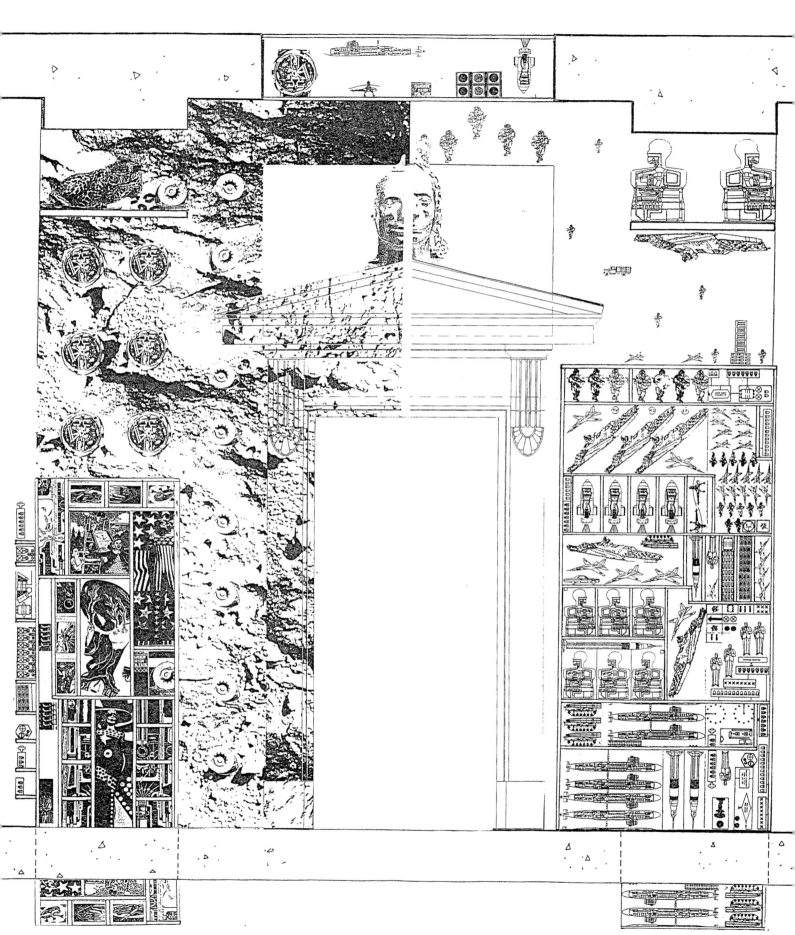

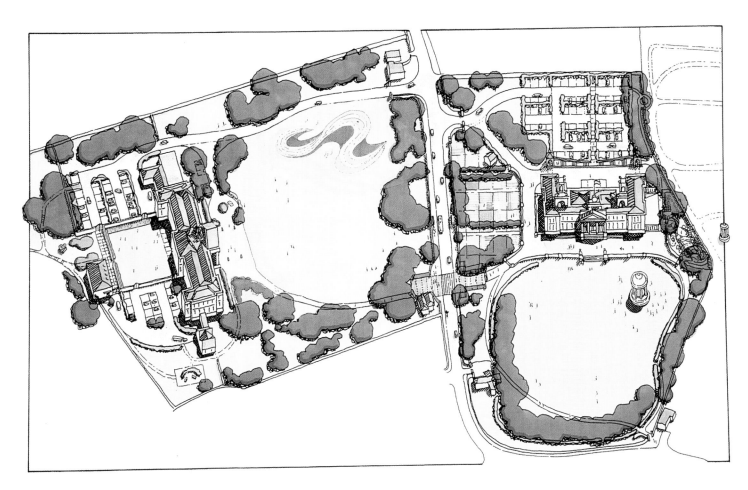

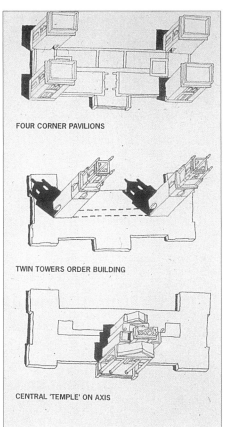

FOUR CORNER PAVILIONS

TWIN TOWERS ORDER BUILDING

CENTRAL 'TEMPLE' ON AXIS

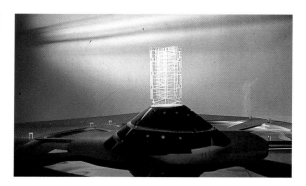

Northumberland Cross

The Northumberland Cross has been devised as a cathedral for the modern age. The building will have special significance in marking the role of St Cuthbert, among others in north-east England, in the spread of Christianity through Europe during the Dark Ages. In this fusion of past and future, religion is reconciled with technological advances.

Three spaces offer different ways of experiencing the building. The first, the cross, is a structural tour de force made almost entirely of glass. The second is a continually revolving platform incorporating the arena. The third is a static undercarriage containing exhibitions. Above the revolving arena will be a large cathedral-like space for performance and

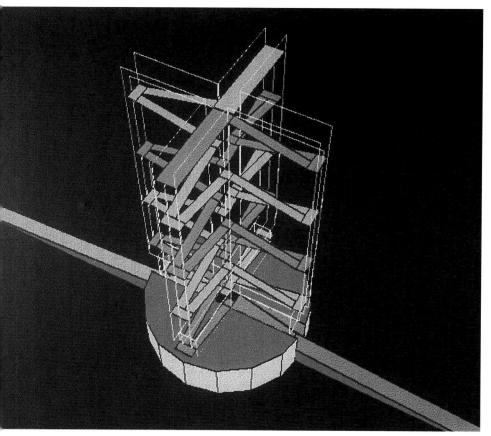

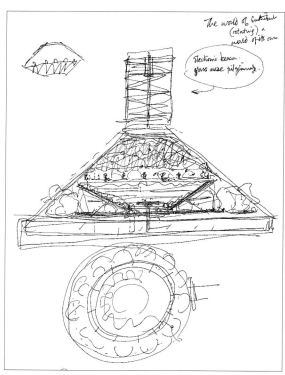

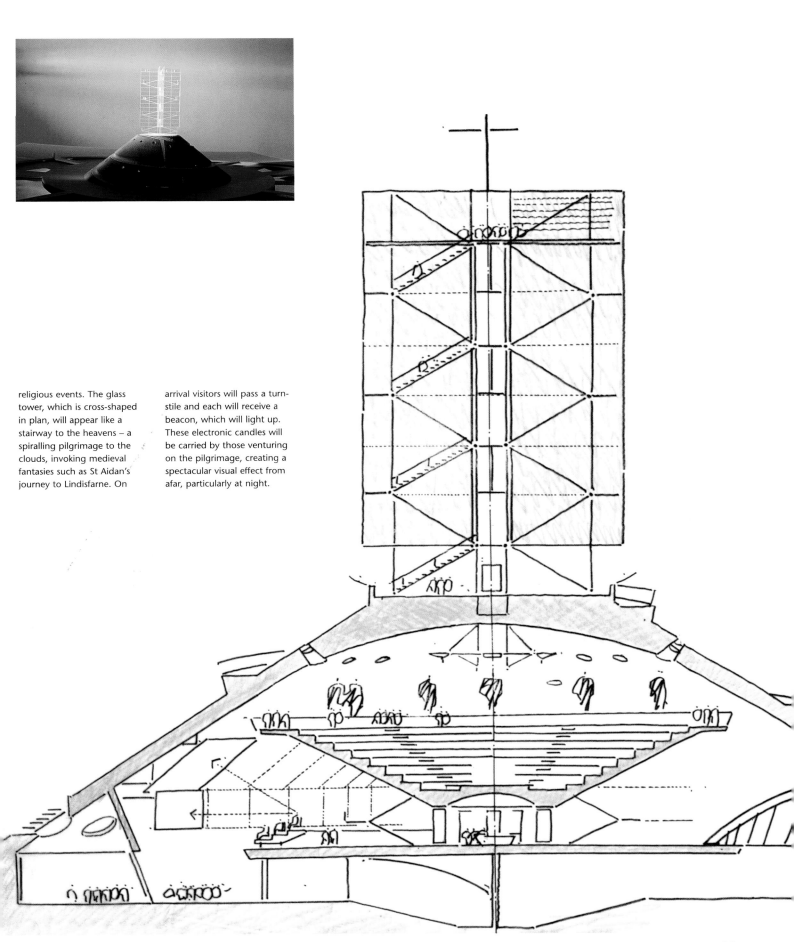

religious events. The glass tower, which is cross-shaped in plan, will appear like a stairway to the heavens – a spiralling pilgrimage to the clouds, invoking medieval fantasies such as St Aidan's journey to Lindisfarne. On arrival visitors will pass a turnstile and each will receive a beacon, which will light up. These electronic candles will be carried by those venturing on the pilgrimage, creating a spectacular visual effect from afar, particularly at night.

Sheraton Health Club Edinburgh

The masterplan for Edinburgh's new financial district is focussed on a public space completely surrounded by new buildings. In order to make this an inviting place, something was required which would draw people to it for reasons other than work. A restaurant and shops were the obvious choices, but the location of the site – between the Conference Centre and the existing Sheraton Hotel – suggested an additional function which could form an annexe to the hotel and allow guests to pass through. A health club was proposed, incorporating the latest ideas in spa features.

The building contains restaurants and shops at the Conference Square level, with the two-storey health club above. The pool is located on the top level and the gym on the reception level, with the changing rooms on a half level in-between. This creates a sequence along which the other functions are located, with the 'split' widened to make a central entrance hall.

This creates a block which is predominantly solid on the north side and a block which is predominantly glazed on the south side. These blocks are unified visually by a folding frame of reconstituted stone, which also frames views through the building from the Conference Centre to the hotel. The frame also functions as an ordering device for the exuberance of the elevations, intended to enliven and give focus to Conference Square.

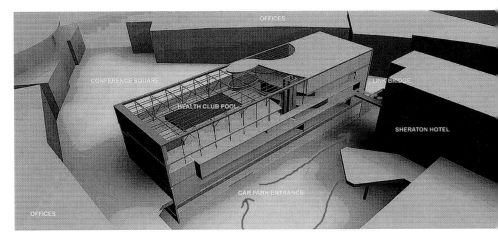

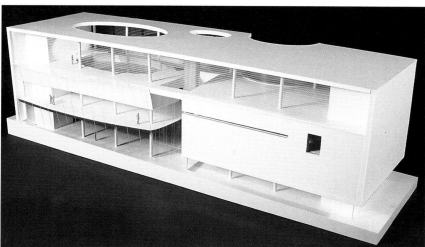

The health club programme suggested a split between private space which is enclosed and solid, and shared space which is open and light. The solid side becomes massive cracked rock. The light side plays with transparency and shifting fractures of glass. Together they are clasped by a massive folding plane, seemingly peeled from the surface of Conference Square.

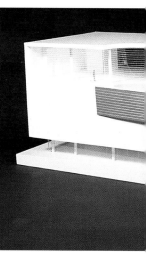

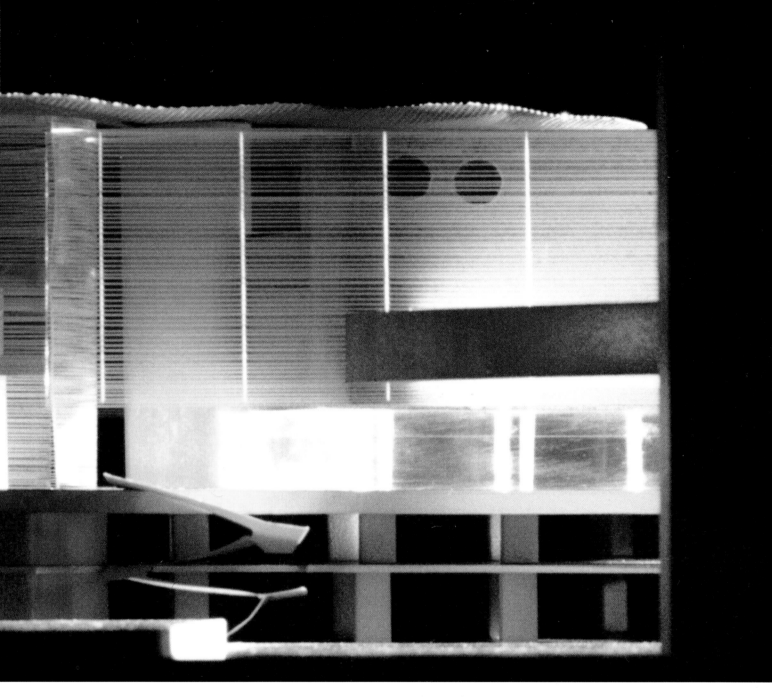

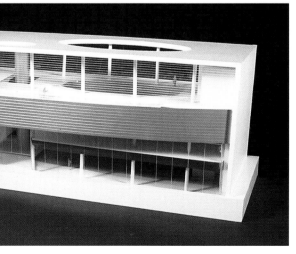

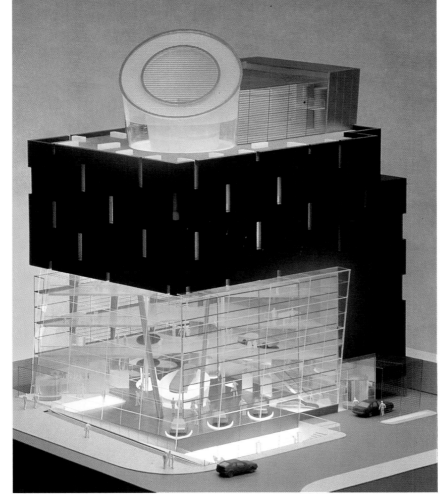

Headquarters Building, Korea

This building brings together an intriguing mix of uses associated with the rich diversity of modern urban and corporate life – an exhibition space, cafe and restaurant, health care facilities, secretariat and offices for the company chairman. A simple cubic volume placed on the site becomes a unifying and symbolic form representing the company. The elegant composition of glass (clear, translucent and opaque) and louvres on a skeletal metal frame accommodates the varied programme within. The building will feature advanced intelligent environmental technologies – an appropriate metaphor for the client's high tech computer business.

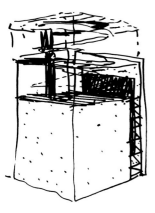

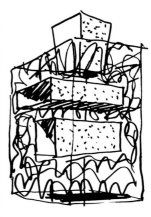

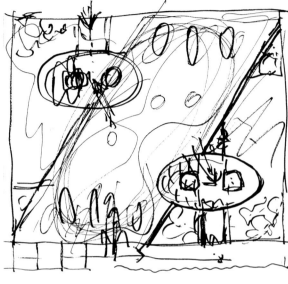

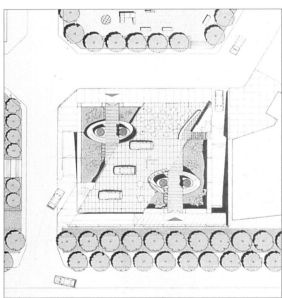

This related scheme brings together the traditional requirements of a residence with the particular requirements of the business and social commitments of the client, a prominent public figure. The design is intended to reflect an image appropriate to the new spirit and vision of the client and his family, and provide a modern and sophisticated response to the site and its location.

International Centre for Life
Newcastle upon Tyne

One of the UK's 14 Landmark Millennium projects, the £54m International Centre for Life at Newcastle upon Tyne occupies a prominent site next to the main railway station at the western edge of the city centre. The masterplan, which will serve as a catalyst for the renewal of the city's western fringe, forms a framework linking to Grainger Town, the railway lands, the 'theatre village' and west central area.

The architectural approach is based on a collage of ideas and built forms that eschews any singular design concept – a richness which reflects the diversity of the brief. The forms respond to the urban context yet create sufficient coherence and identity to establish a focal point. A major new public space, Times Square, incorporates the historic market keeper's house as a cafe and information facility.

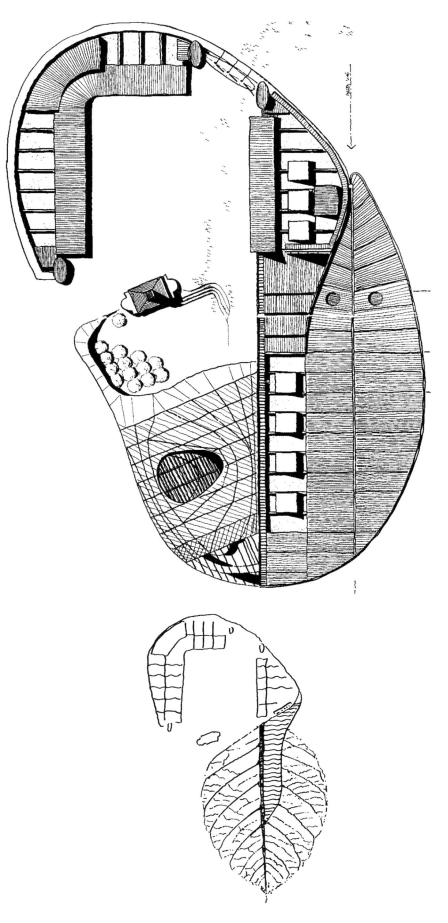

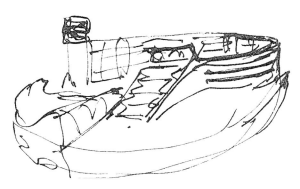

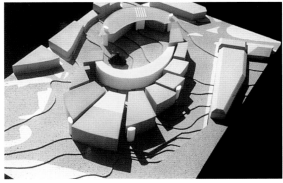

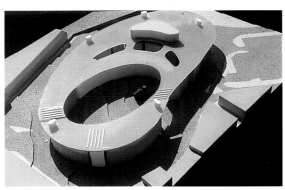

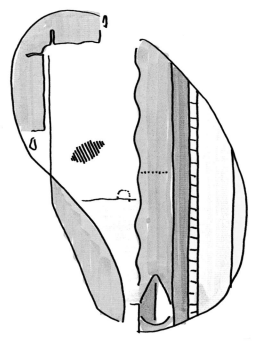

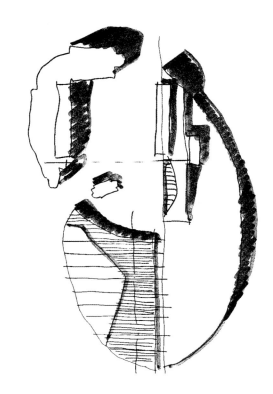

Labels within the central plan:

WESTMORLAND ROAD.

CENTRAL STATION.

MARLBOROUGH CRES.

BIOSCIENCE BUILDING.

RETAIL

R.
R.
R.
R.
R.
R.
R.
R.

GENETICS INSTITUTE

MILLENNIUM SQUARE.

LOADING.

LOADING.

RAMP.

VISITOR ATTRACTION.

CONT.

TEMP. EXHIB GALLERY 1.

SECTION

EDUCATION.

INTRO GALLERY ORIENTATION.

GALLERY.

GALLERY.

GALLERY.

RAILWAY STREET.

ADMINISTRATION.

GALLERY.

AUDITORIUM.

RAMP.

TECHNICAL UNDER.

FORTH ST.

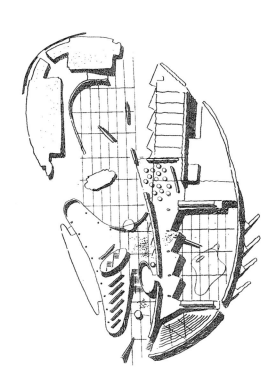

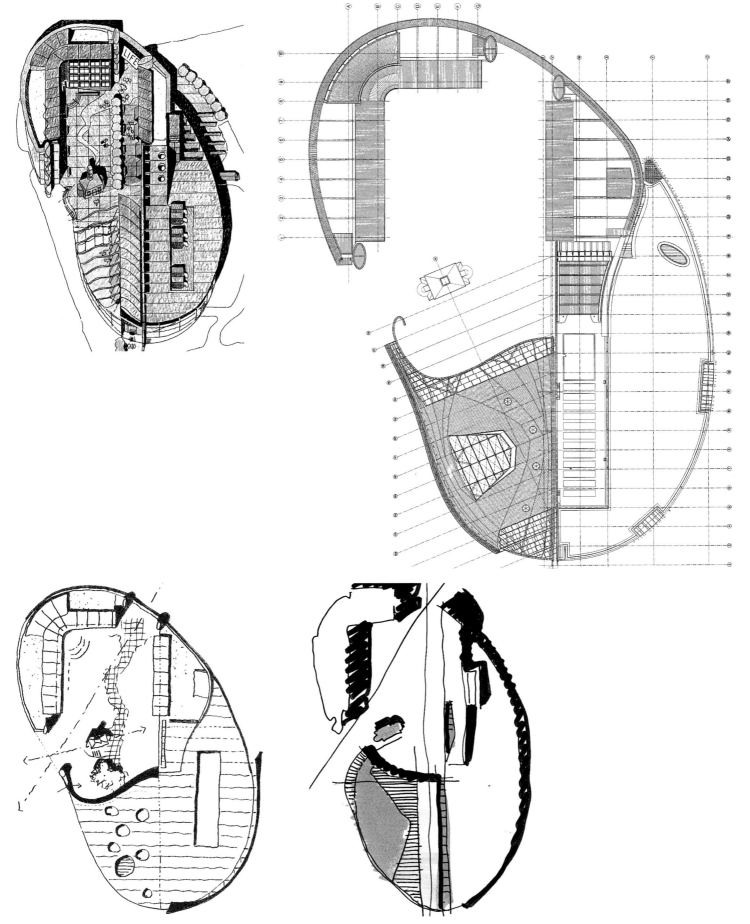

41

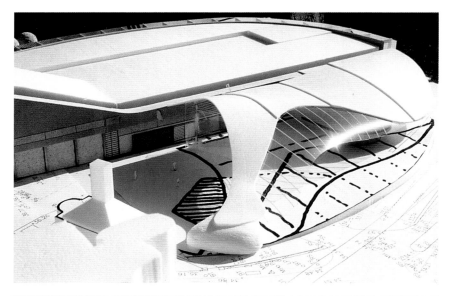

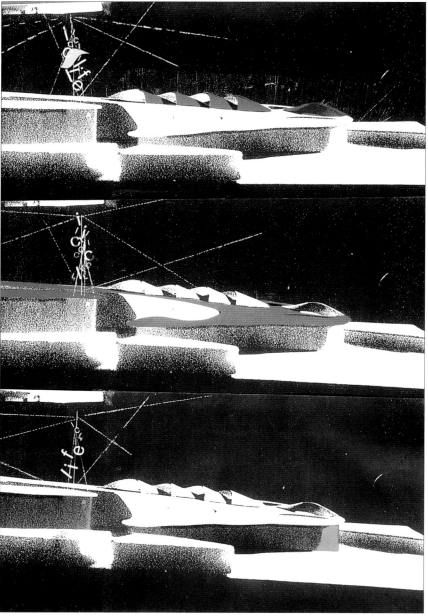

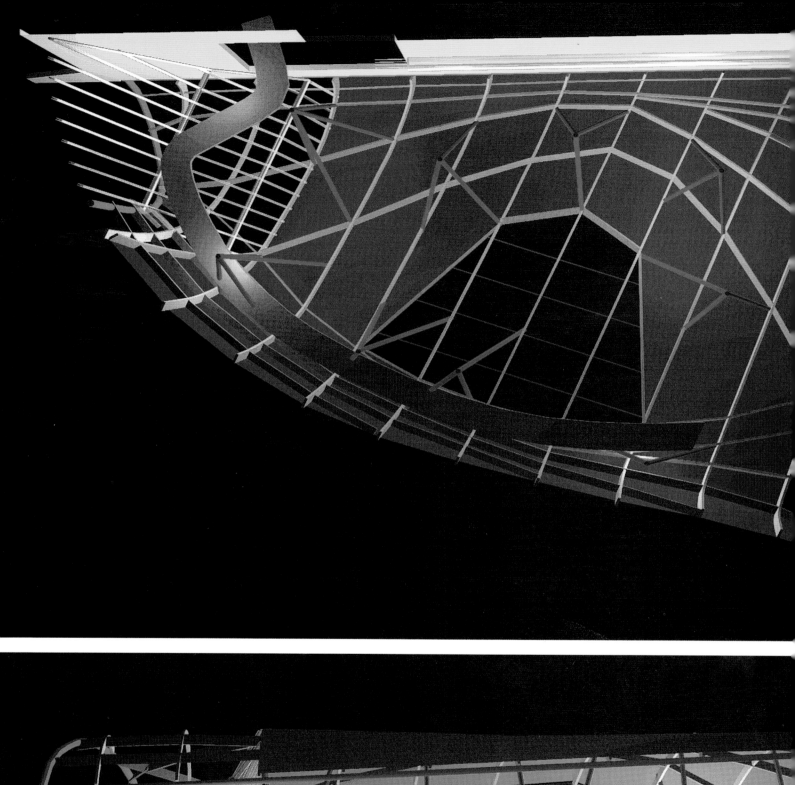
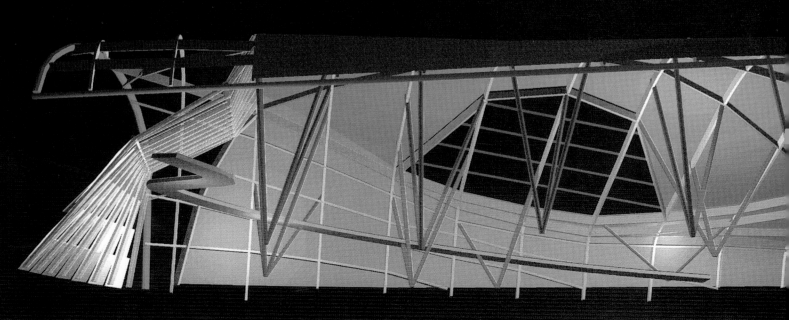

The most powerful visual image of Helix, the wave-form roof over the entrance and daylit part of the exhibition area, provides a transitional space between the new urban square and the darkened exhibition galleries and education facilities. The visitor route forms a fundamental part of the masterplan, creating future linkages to adjoining development sites. The main galleries are a flexible 'black box' providing large clear-span areas for the heavily themed exhibition. The palette of materials to be employed for Helix includes timber, render, pre-patinated copper roofing, profile metal cladding and curtain walling. A large media wall facing the main railway lines announces the scheme to people arriving in or passing through Newcastle, while a skysign and double-helix light sculpture firmly establish the design on the city skyline.

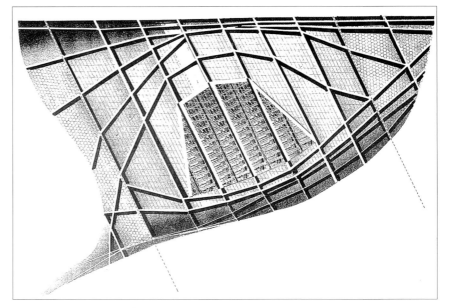

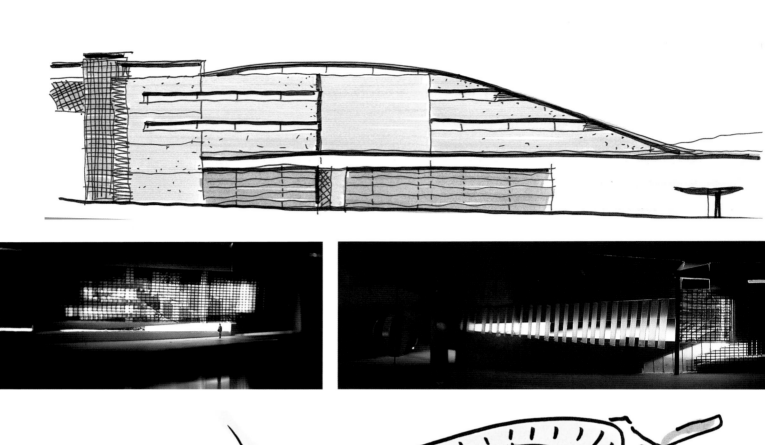

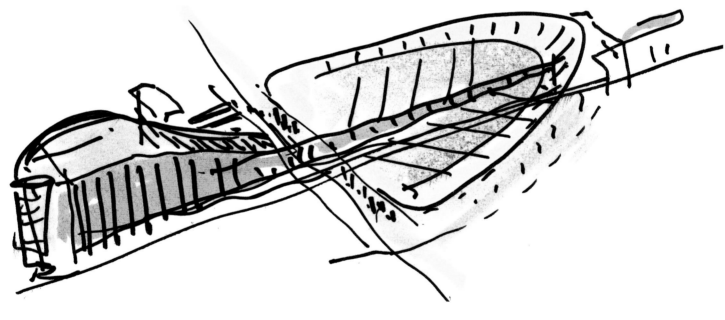

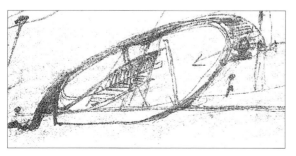

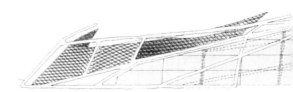

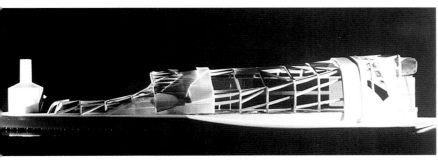

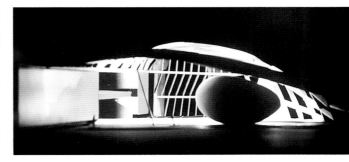

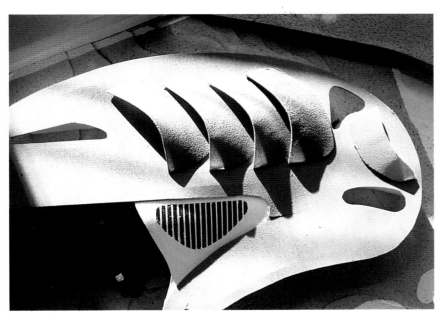

The International Centre for Life brings together on one site a number of distinctive elements:

• Helix (9100m²). A futuristic and interactive themed indoor family entertainment centre accommodating up to 300,000 visitors per year, Helix will explore DNA, how it works and what it means for human beings.

• Genetics Institute (5,400m²). A human genetics research centre accommodating more than 150 academic and specialist clinical consulting service staff. The institute will provide clinical applications for genetic research and act as a major centre for fundamental research into inherited diseases including cystic fibrosis and muscular dystrophy, infectious diseases, cancer and heart disease.

• The Bio Science Centre (8000m²). Specialist commercial laboratory and office space designed for small to medium sized companies in the biotechnology sector.

• Retail accommodation (2,000m²).

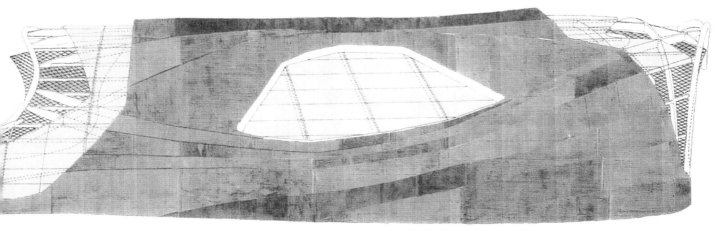

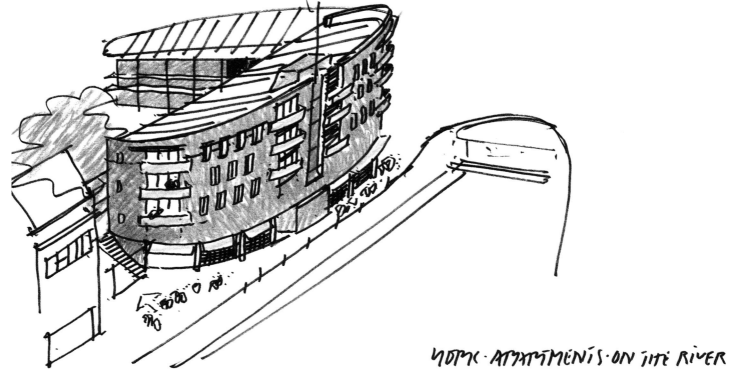

YORK · APARTMENTS · ON THE RIVER

Castlegate
York

This mixed-use development lies south of York's central shopping district, within the historic core conservation area and in an area of archaeological importance. Adjacent to the Coppergate shopping centre, Jorvik Centre and the castle, it is the main point of entry for most visitors to the city. Following an architectural competition in 1991, Terry Farrell & Partners have worked with Wimpey Property Holdings, Land Securities Properties and the city council on the masterplan and detailed proposals.

The proposals combine a wide range of uses, including retail, residential, office and leisure, in addition to a new Crown Court building which will address and complement the existing museum square. The scheme is intended to be both well mannered and contextual, with a traditional street pattern which repairs the urban grain of the city and enhances the setting of the surrounding buildings.

The retail component comprises a major department store (9,000m²) situated between Piccadilly and the River Foss, along with additional retail space (3,000m²). Primary pedestrian routes connect the scheme with the adjoining Coppergate shopping centre, with a range of smaller retail units and kiosks at ground level. The existing Fenwick store in St Mary's Square will be extended to further complement the proposals. A terrace of 123 residential units will form a new frontage to Piccadilly, relating in scale to the historic Walmgate residential area to the east. Small office suites will occupy the upper floors of the buildings beside the castle museum, with further accommodation for leisure and cultural use (12,000m²).

"THE MODERN WAY OF BUILDING MUST BE FLEXIBLE + VIGOROUS. EVEN SMART AND HARD. WE MUST GIVE UP DESIGNING THE BROKEN DOWN PICTURESQUE WHICH IS PART OF THE IDEAL OF MAKE BELIEVE. THE ENEMY IS NOT SCIENCE BUT VULGARITY, A PRETENCE TO BEAUTY AT SECOND HAND. WE HAVE TO AWAKEN THE CIVIC IDEAL AND AIM FIRST AT THE OBVIOUS COMMONPLACES OF CLEANLINESS, NEATNESS. AND ORDER."
W.R. LETHABY · 1911.

YORK · CASTLEGATE MASTERPLAN · JULY ·97· T·FARRELL ·

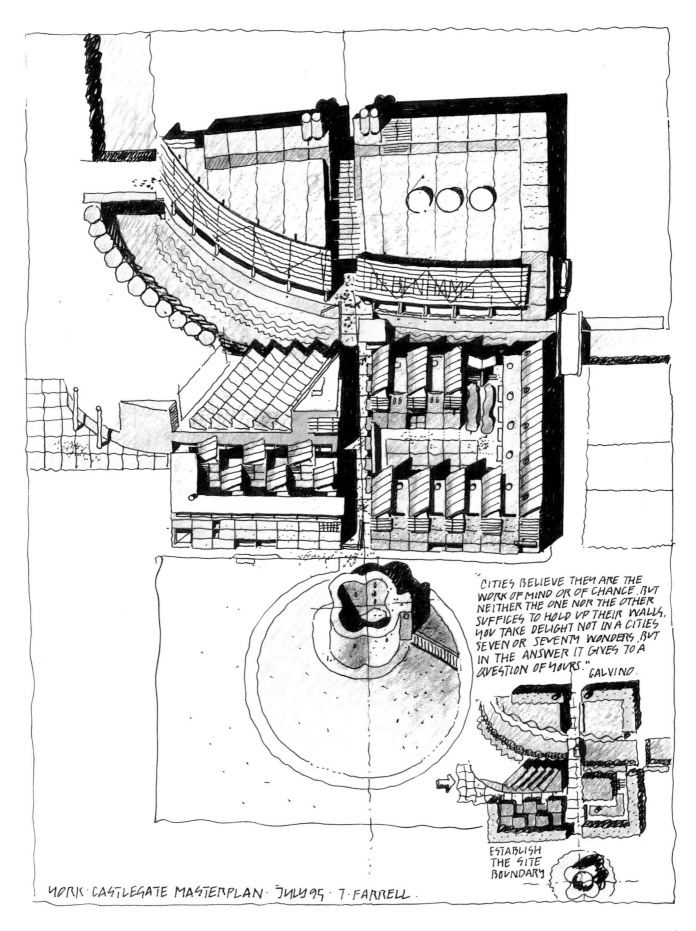

"CITIES BELIEVE THEY ARE THE
WORK OF MIND OR OF CHANCE, BUT
NEITHER THE ONE NOR THE OTHER
SUFFICES TO HOLD UP THEIR WALLS,
YOU TAKE DELIGHT NOT IN A CITIES
SEVEN OR SEVENTY WONDERS, BUT
IN THE ANSWER IT GIVES TO A
QUESTION OF YOURS." CALVINO.

ESTABLISH
THE SITE
BOUNDARY

YORK CASTLEGATE MASTERPLAN · JULY 95 · T FARRELL ·

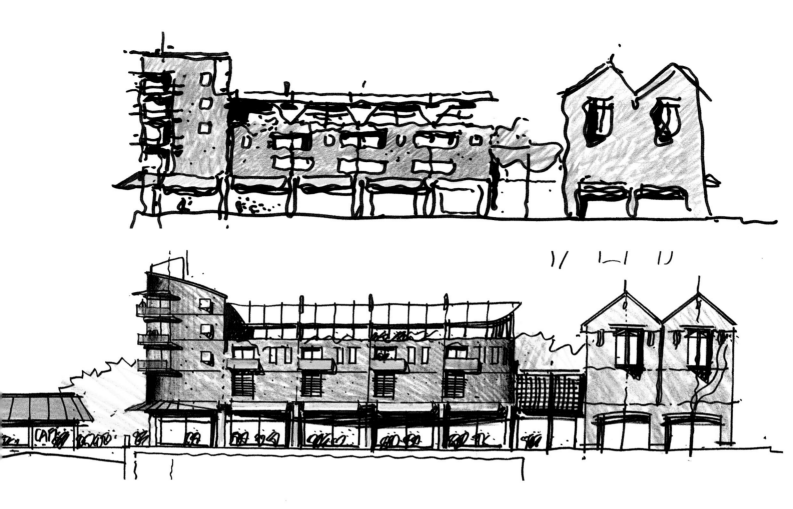

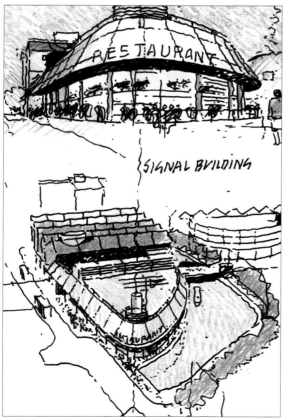

RESTAURANT

SIGNAL BUILDING

In terms of urban design the scheme aims to:

• unify the three separate site areas in a combined development which will repair the urban grain of this important quarter of the city.

• achieve a high quality of both architectural and urban design and link the Castle Precinct and Piccadilly with the city's major shopping and heritage areas.

• revitalise the River Foss and realise its environmental potential by making it a centrepiece of the scheme.

• establish a linked view between Piccadilly and Clifford's Tower.

• create a memorable new civic space which links with the Castle Precinct and acts as a unifying element.

• complete the visual enclosure of the Castle Precinct with buildings of appropriate scale and quality.

• create a sense of unity between old and new by the use of appropriate building materials and landscaping.

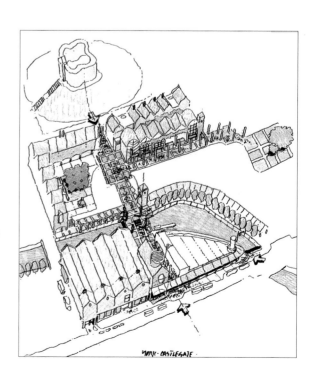

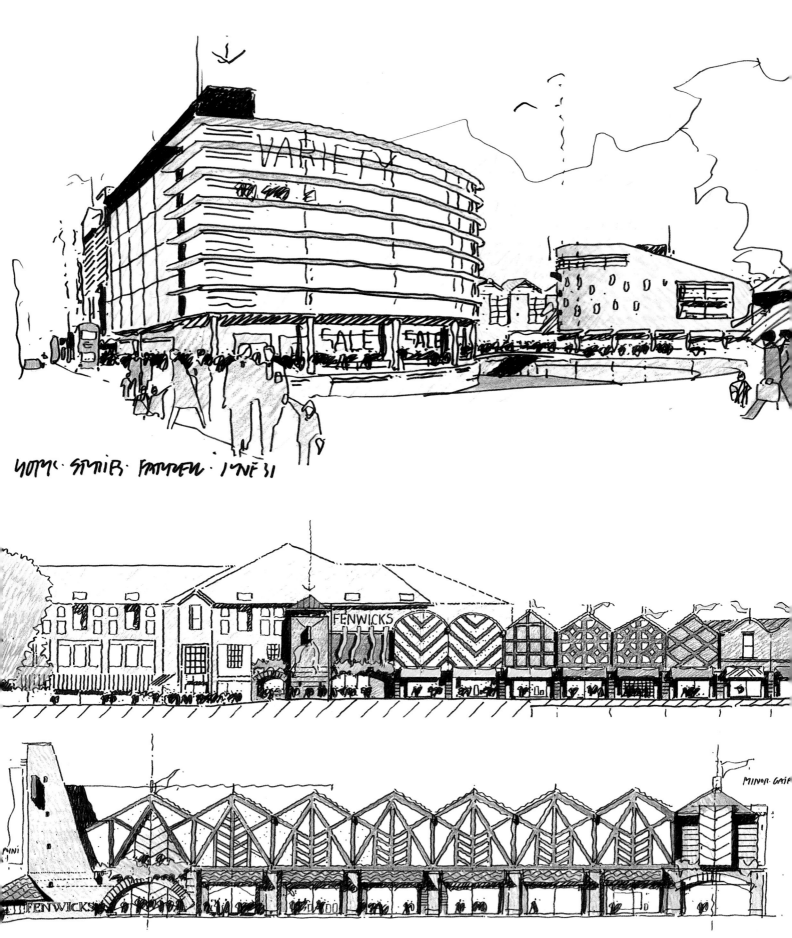

51

THE ROOFLIGHT.

THE BEAM.

THE ROOF.

THE WALL.

BALCONIES

THE TERRACE

Three Quays
London

Three Quays is a landmark four-star hotel of 234 bedrooms, designed for a prominent riverside site and commanding magnificent views of Tower Bridge, the Tower of London and the Thames itself. The building is arranged in response to its unique setting, taking full advantage of the prospect.

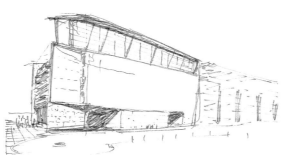

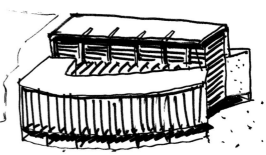

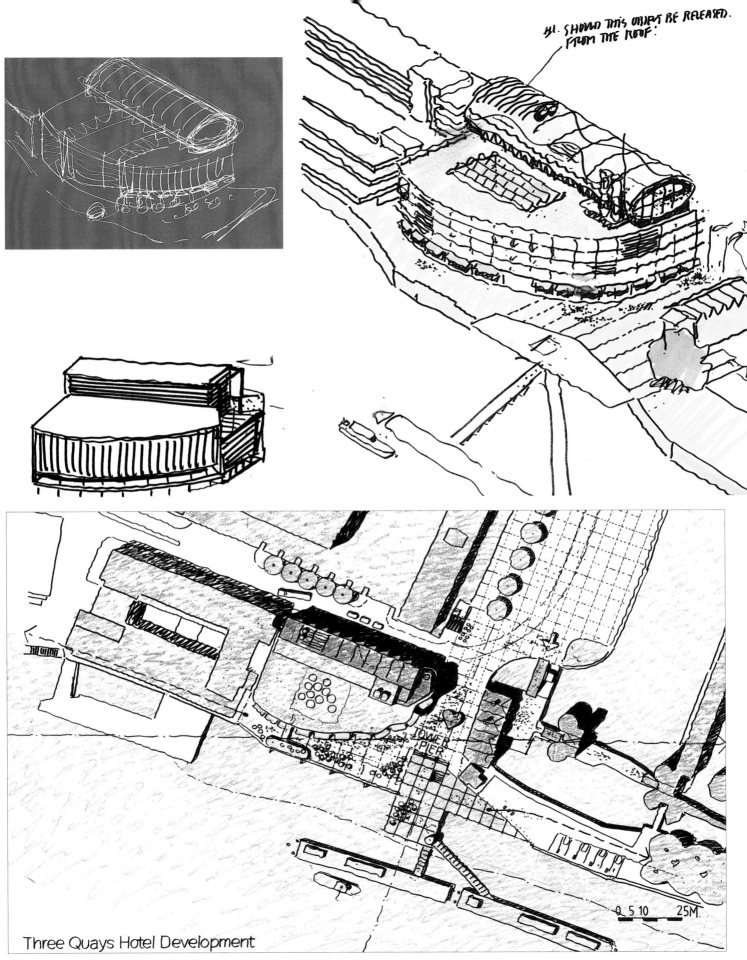

41. SHOULD THIS OBJECT BE RELEASED FROM THE ROOF.

TOWER PIER

0 5 10   25M.

Three Quays Hotel Development

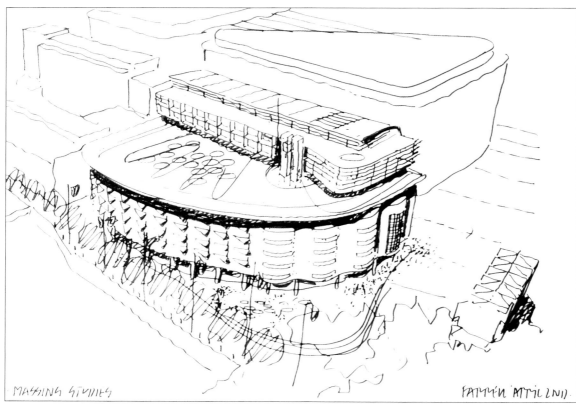

MASSING STUDIES   FATHY'N ATTIL (2ND)

The mass of the building is articulated into two distinct elements, with the principal wavy facade of stone and metal-clad 'Swiss roll' forming rooftop penthouse suites. The plan is arranged on six levels around an atrium with a folding glass roof giving expression to the roofscape. A ring of restaurants, shops and riverside promenade surround the atrium at ground level and create a focus at the core of the building.

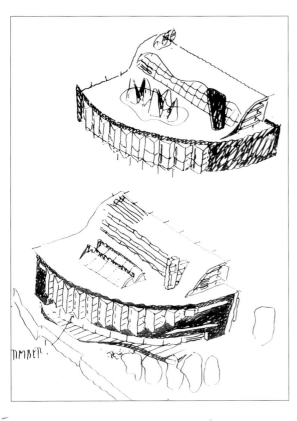

55

Samsung headquarters London

In response to its prominent site near major transportation links, the Samsung headquarters is designed to present a dynamic image from all viewpoints – a striking object in space. The requirements of phase one are consolidated into a single tower at the heart of the site, maximising the area left for future phases – an important aspect of the brief.

The innovative form of the 19-storey tower is an evolutionary development of tried and tested plan forms, with a centralised core and flexible column-free space. Floor plates in the 43,600m² building are generally 2000m², subdivisible into two 1000m² independent units for maximum commercial flexibility.

The building envelope seeks to establish a simple image and strong identity, with a hard shell that protects from traffic noise and integrates active environmental control measures in response to solar orientation. The tower is arranged around a central atrium which opens towards the park, creating a strong visual link between landscape and the heart of the building.

The base contains public spaces, reception, marketing and education facilities; the middle zone contains the world of work and endeavour; and the top contains welfare and executive functions.

A subsequent phase would include further office space and training accommodation related to training facilities. The long-term development plan aims to achieve a full working community for the twenty-first century – an important part of the client's globalisation plans.

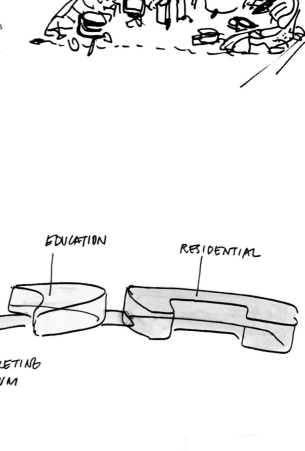

ALT. (PHASE 2)

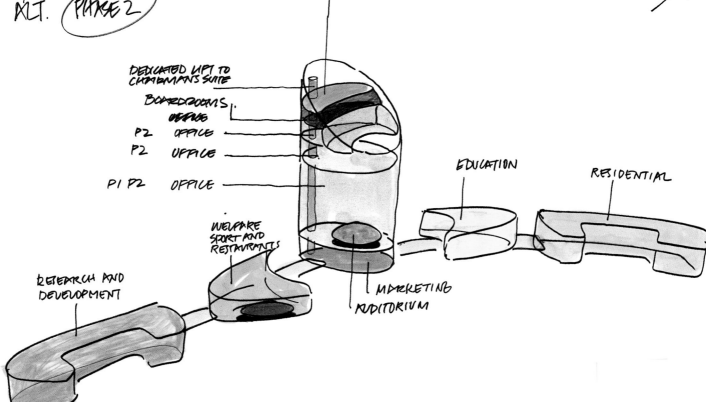

DEDICATED LIFT TO
CHAIRMANS SUITE

BOARDROOMS
OFFICE

P2   OFFICE

P2   OFFICE

P1 P2   OFFICE

WELFARE
SPORT AND
RESTAURANTS

RESEARCH AND
DEVELOPMENT

MARKETING

AUDITORIUM

EDUCATION

RESIDENTIAL

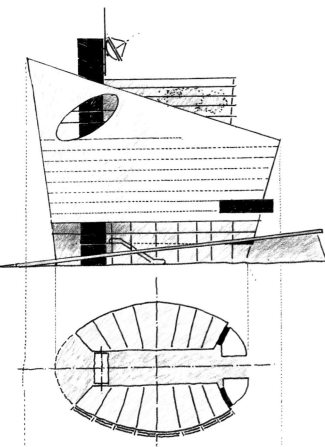
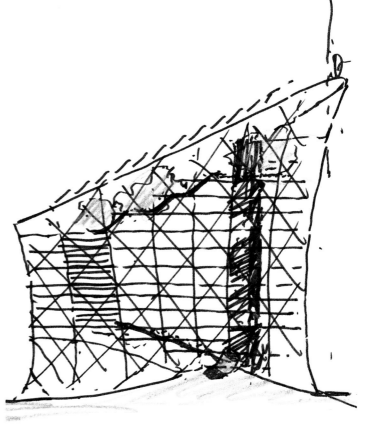

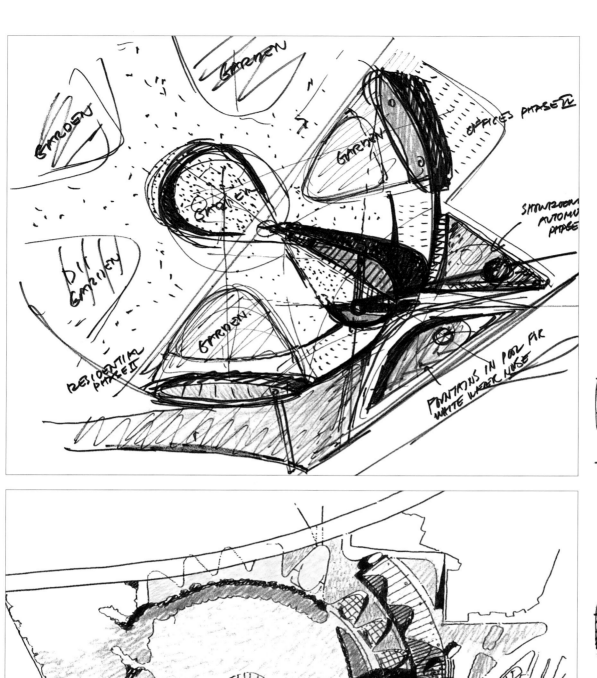

GARDEN

GARDEN

GARDEN

GARDEN

DU GARDEN

GARDEN

GARDEN

OFFICES PHASE IV

SHOWROOM AUTOMO PHASE

RESIDENTIAL PHASE II

FOUNTAINS IN POOL FIR WHITE WATER NOISE

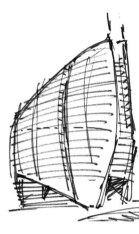

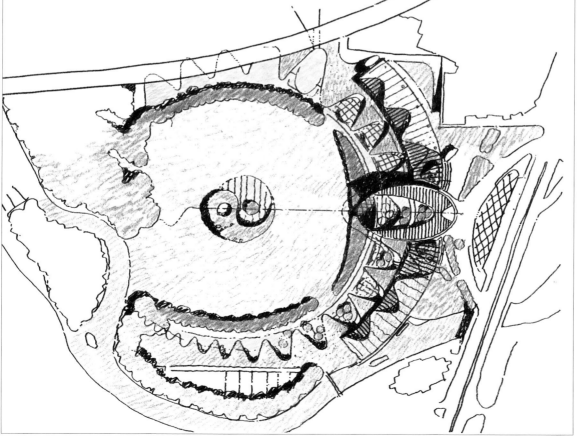

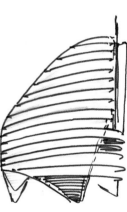

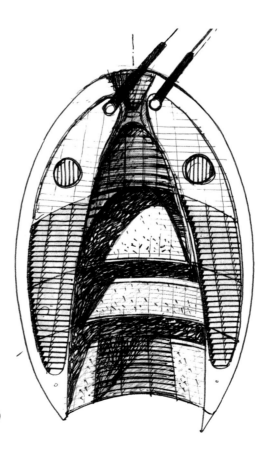

The split plan generates a symbolic 'gateway' axis linking east and west – the urban frontage to the parkland setting. The oval plan form, which combines high-tech with natural forms, achieves a good ratio of floor area to external wall, reducing both the capital cost of external cladding and the energy requirement.

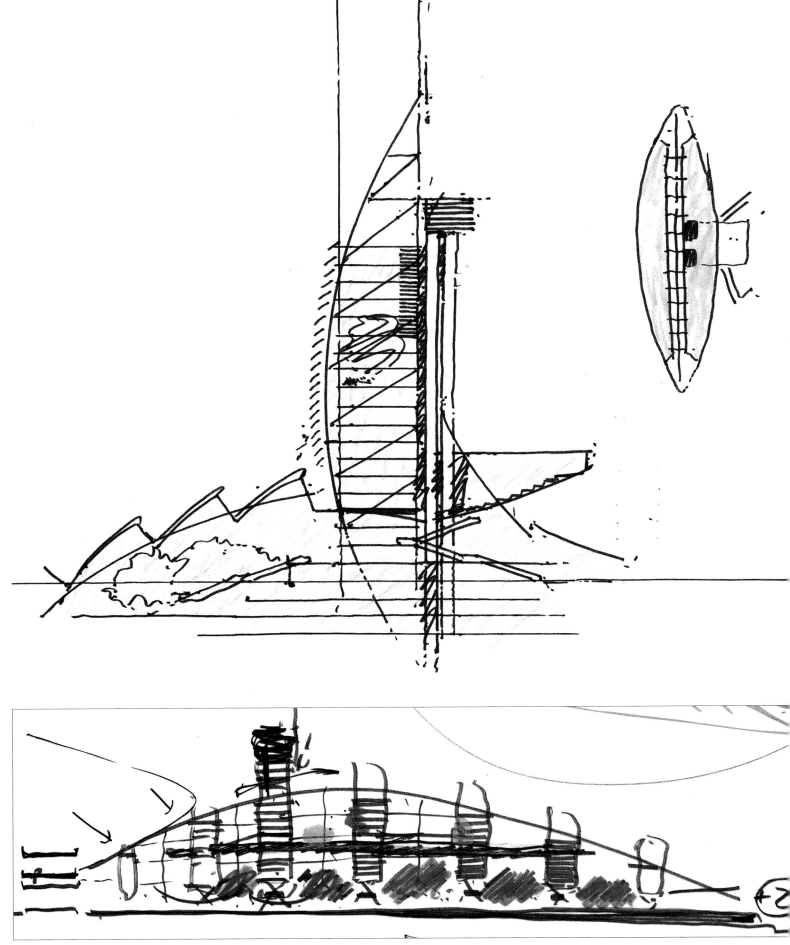

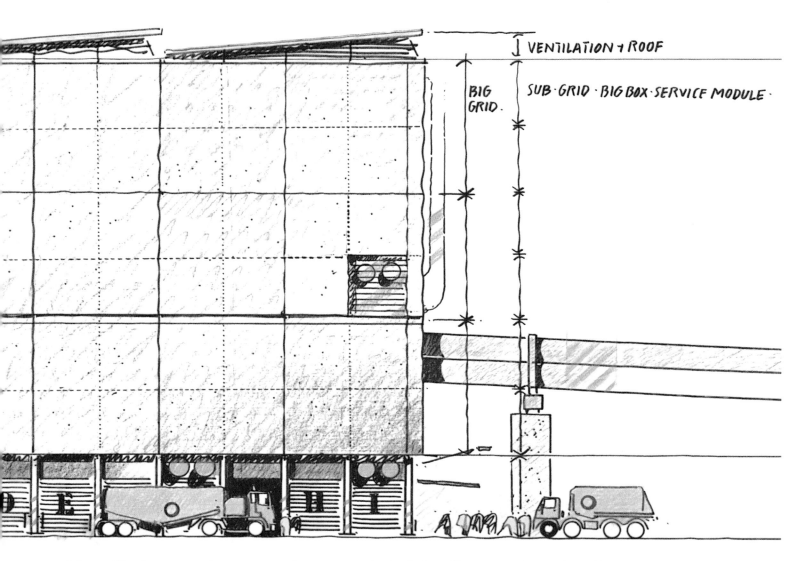

VENTILATION + ROOF

BIG GRID.

SUB·GRID·BIG BOX·SERVICE MODULE·

Blue Circle Kent

Large structures such as viaducts, power stations and bridges celebrate the dynamic relationship between built form and the landscape. Elegant and poetic solutions can be created which fully integrate architectural and engineering disciplines – ie objects in the landscape, sculpted and enhanced by form, light and colour.

The extraction of chalk is equally heroic in scale, a sophisticated process requiring a variety of plant configurations. A number of objectives for Medway Cement Works were established early on:

• reconciliation of scale – the need to provide transitions between the context and the intervention in terms of built form, architectural language, colour and materials.

• composition – control and ordering of the visual characteristics of the works when viewed from near and far and elevated vantage points.

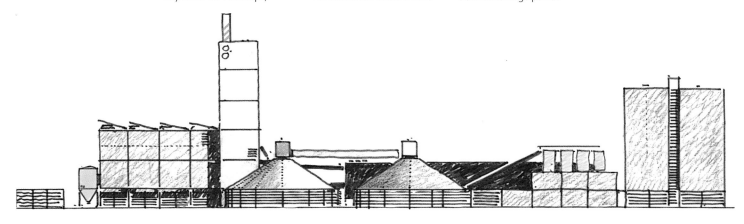

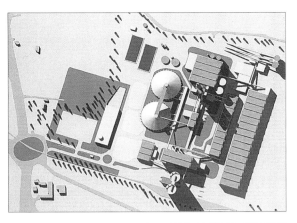

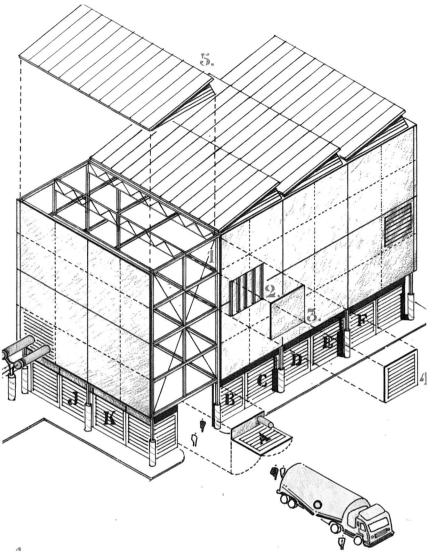

• hierarchy of forms – the design recognises the importance of unifying an inherently disparate collection of engineering process components.
• landscape – a fully integrated landscape design reinforces the architectural and engineering disciplines.

The architectural approach to dealing with the large forms has been to enhance their vertical proportions and control their visual bulk by means of semi-transparent screens. The pre-heater tower is designed to function as a 'landscape marker' in the rural setting in the same vein as a cathedral tower.

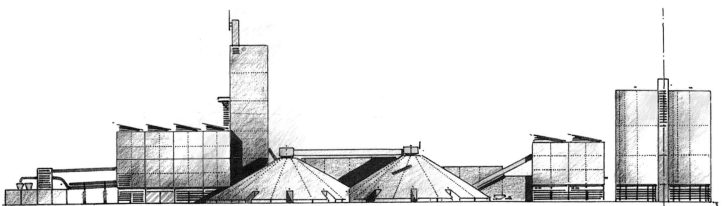

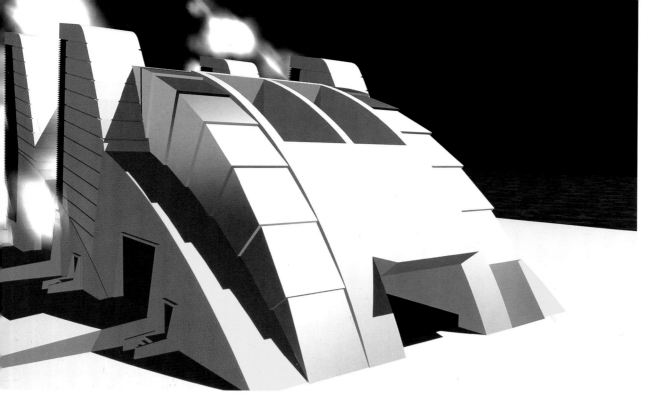

Kowloon Ventilation Building, Hong Kong

The Kowloon Ventilation Building is one of a series of buildings containing mechanical and electrical equipment for the rail-link connecting the city of Hong Kong to the new Chek Lap Kok airport. It contains floodgates, power transformers and ventilation units and sits in a large public park overlooking the harbour. Because of the prominence of the site, a landmark building of high quality was required. The organic design – visually strong but sympathetic to its setting – is based on an undulating form relating to both the rolling landscape and the waves of the adjacent harbour. The surrounding landscape and harbourscape has been designed to echo and enhance the shape of the building.

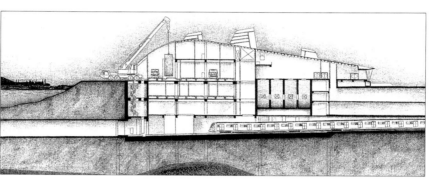

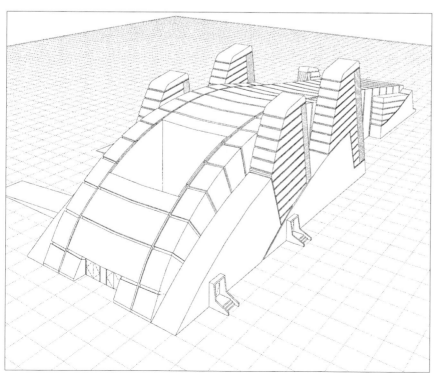

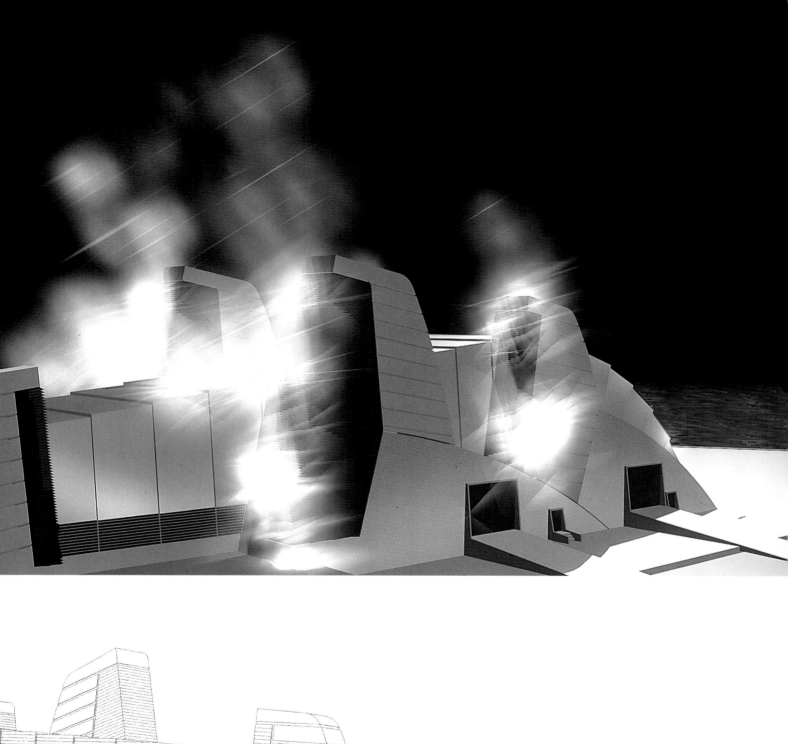
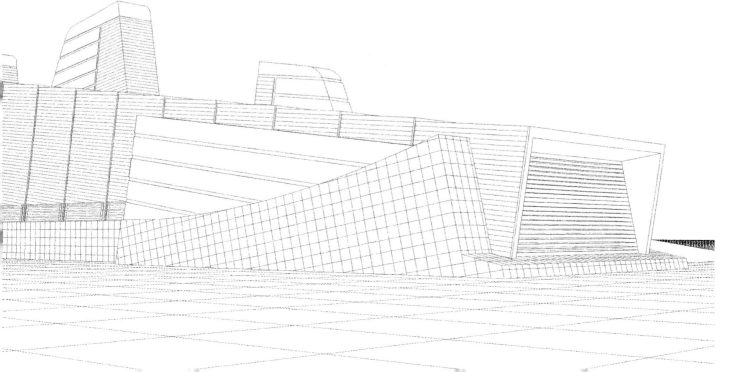

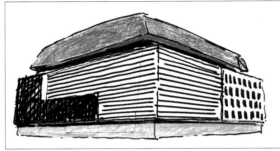

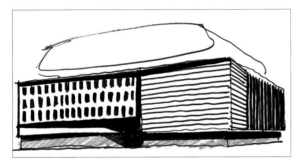

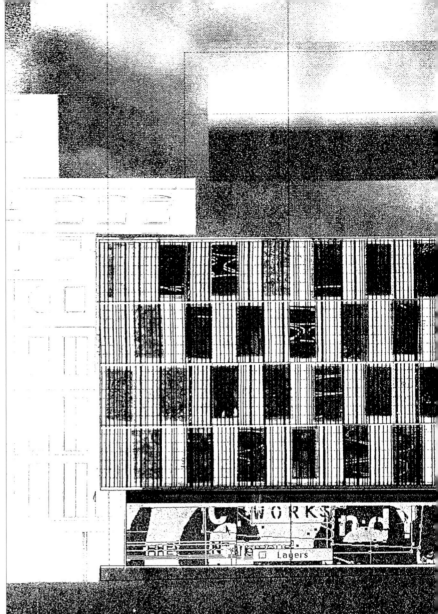

Mayfair Place
London

This scheme is intended to maximise the unique opportunities of an island site in Mayfair, a stone's throw from the Ritz and Berkeley Square. Developed as a single office building, the project seeks to emphasise the site's identity as a whole, creating a 'place' as opposed to four streets with four elevations.

The block is modelled with a strong horizontal emphasis. An open ground plane of activity (restaurants, retail etc) supports four storeys of office space with an unexpectedly expressive rooftop. Two cornice lines create an elevation datum, within which the office space becomes a series of interlocking volumes. This reinforces the singular identity but allows individual elevations to be contextual.

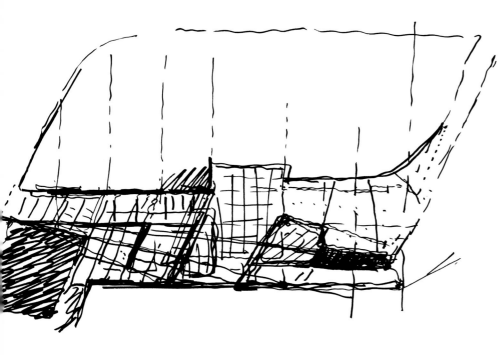

Retail and Clinic Buildings, Seoul

These two buildings stand on a new campus of museums, sports facilities and clinics to be built by a major Korean corporation. Located on a hillside in a prestigious residential district of Seoul, the campus has been masterplanned by Rem Koolhaas, with buildings by a range of architects including Terry Farrell, Mario Botta and Jean Nouvel, as well as Koolhaas himself.

The retail and clinic buildings define a gateway to the complex. The former acts as a large glazed billboard to the main road while the stepped form of the clinic responds to the displaced strata of the hillside and the hilltop museum.

each layer entirely its own character very diff. fortunes etc.

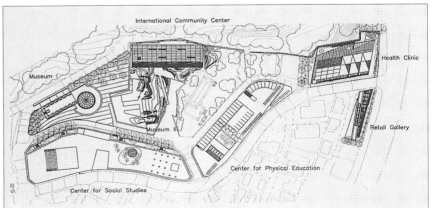

International Community Center

Health Clinic

Museum I

Museum II

Retail Gallery

Center for Physical Education

Center for Social Studies

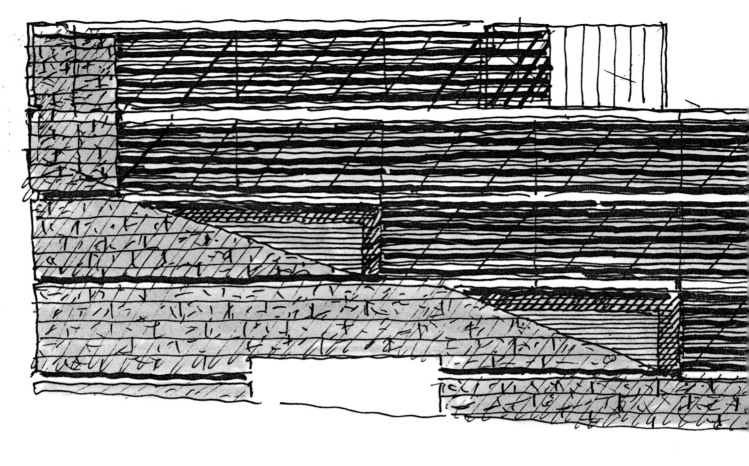

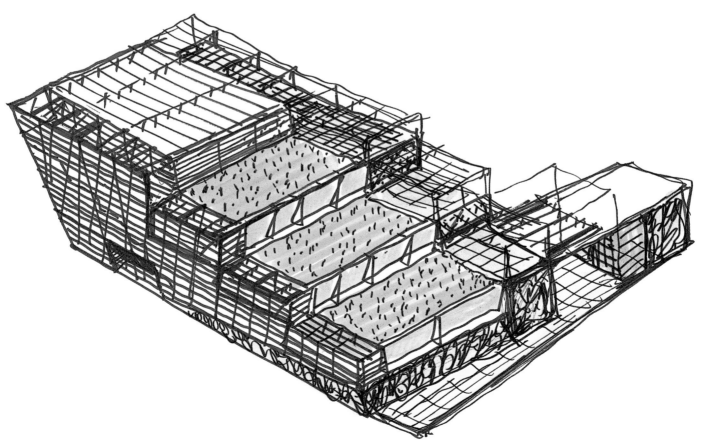

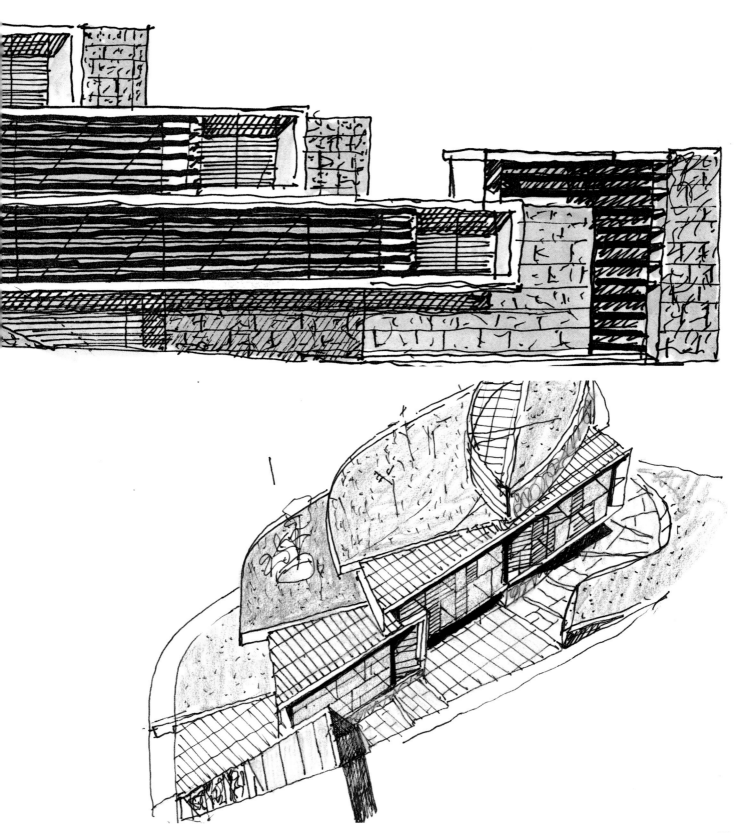

SMSUNG · HPUDJEST · MUSEUM SHOP·   FARREN·DEC95

SAMSUNG · H · PROJECT ·   FARREN · DEC 95 ·

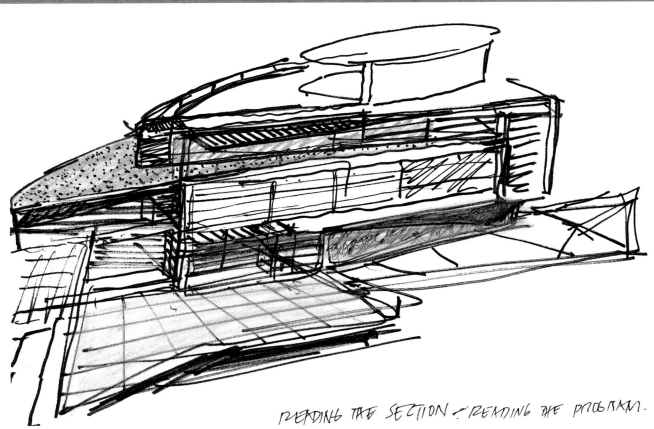

READING THE SECTION = READING THE PROGRAM.

75

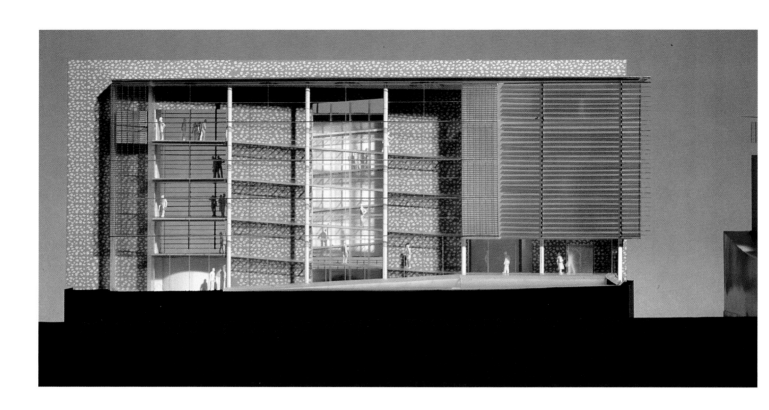

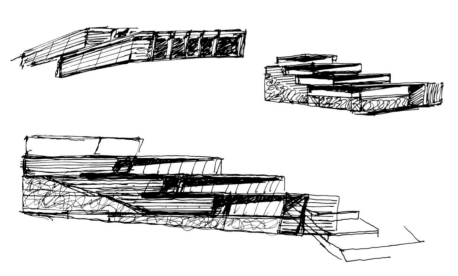

The clinic, which will focus on internal medicine and sensorial diseases, serves as a satellite to the company's main medical centre. Pedestrian access is through a stepped communal garden to the north which is also used as an alternative route into the complex.

The retail building is a flexible facility which can accommodate exhibitions and other events. The open floor plates of the exhibition spaces and the ramped internal circulation behind the four-storey glazed wall are clearly visible from the road.

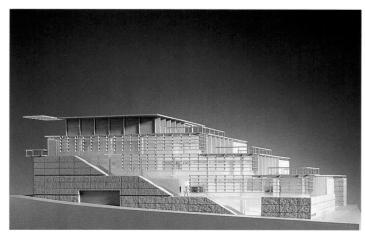

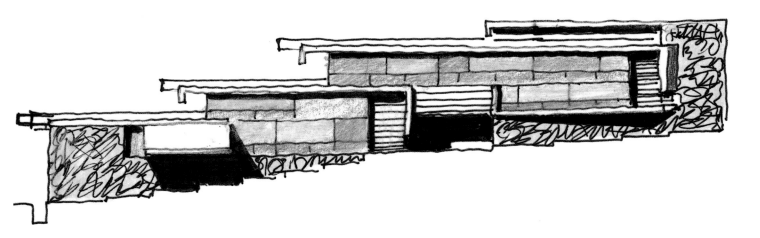

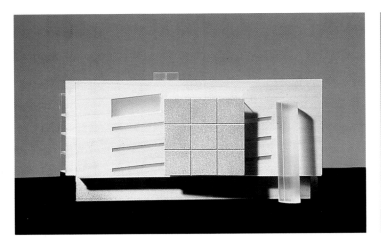

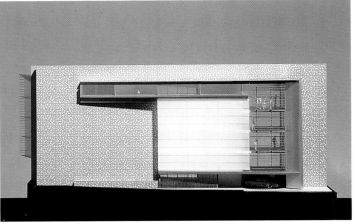

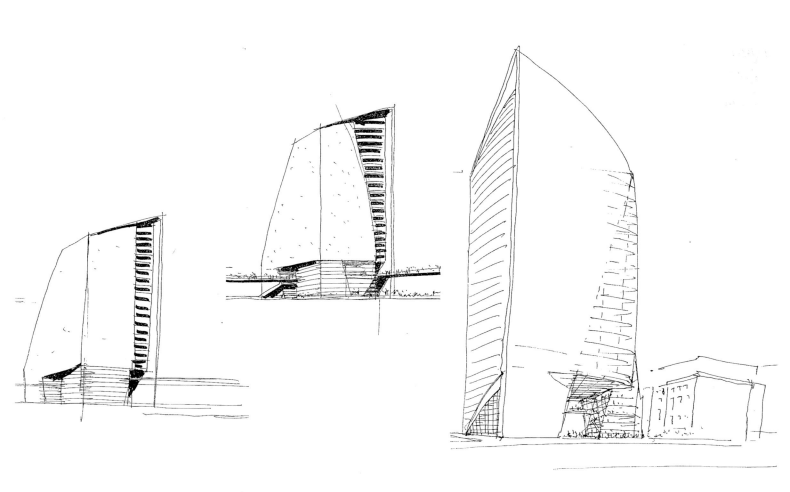
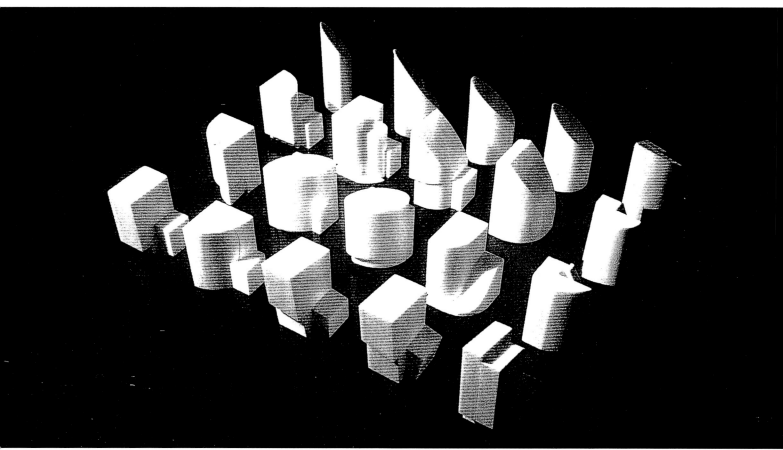

Moor House
London

This proposed 20-storey tower in the City of London is characterised by its striking sloping silhouette and simple elevational planes. These sculptural qualities create a landmark building with a dynamic image clearly visible along London Wall and within the broader cityscape. This approach is consistent with the tower's strategic location at the Moorgate transportation node, where it provides a new civic space and a gateway to the elevated city walkway, Moorgate and potential Crossrail interchanges.

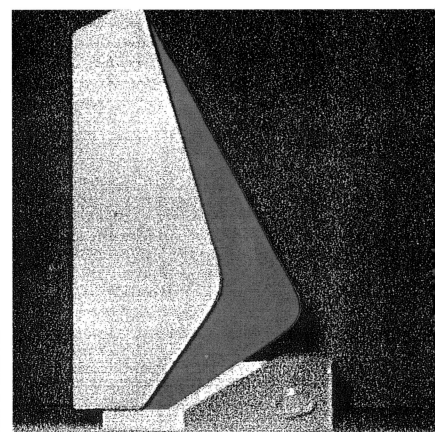

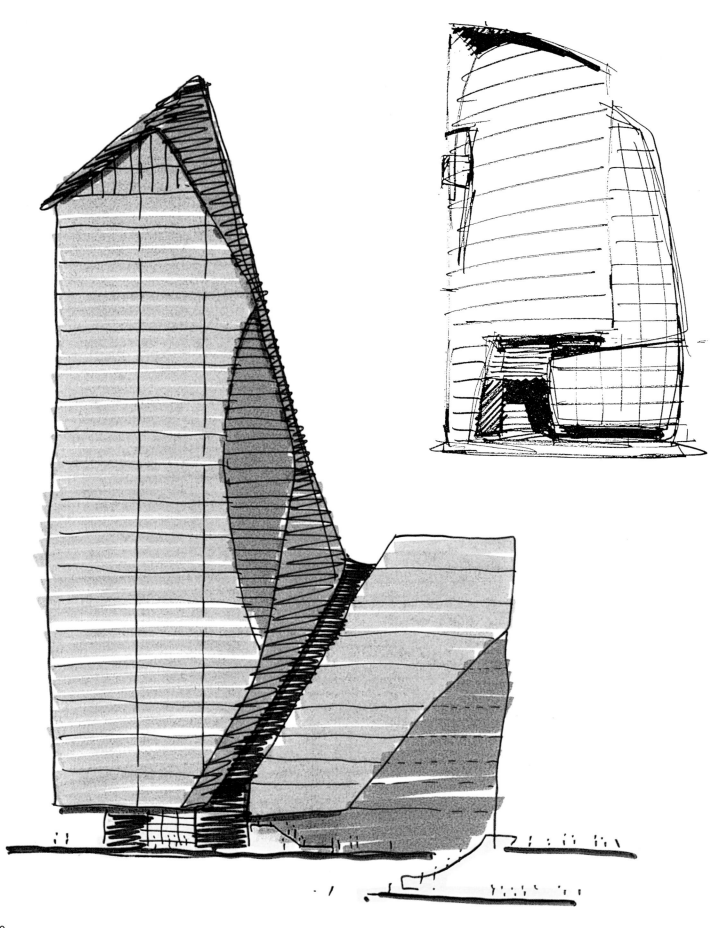

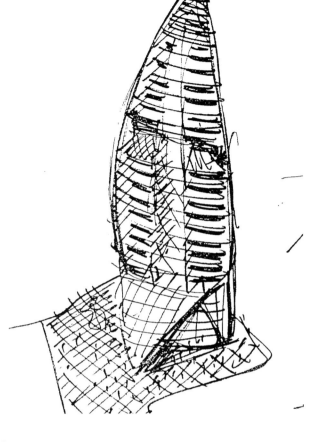

The building form has been developed in direct response to the site constraints and the commercial brief, with particular consideration of rights of light to the neighbouring buildings and the St Paul's cathedral sightlines. The building skin is envisaged as a series of simple clean planes which respond to their solar and urban orientation.

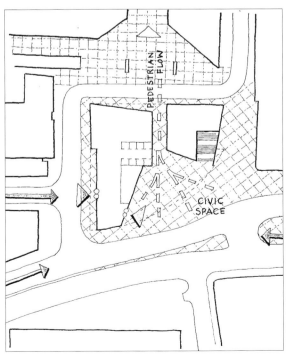

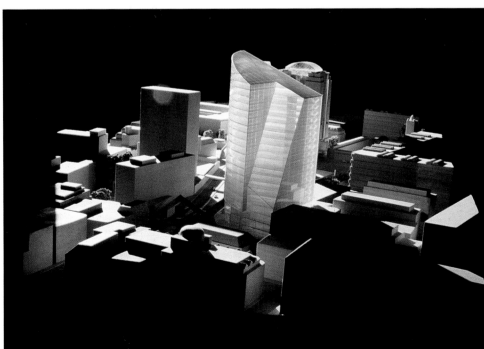

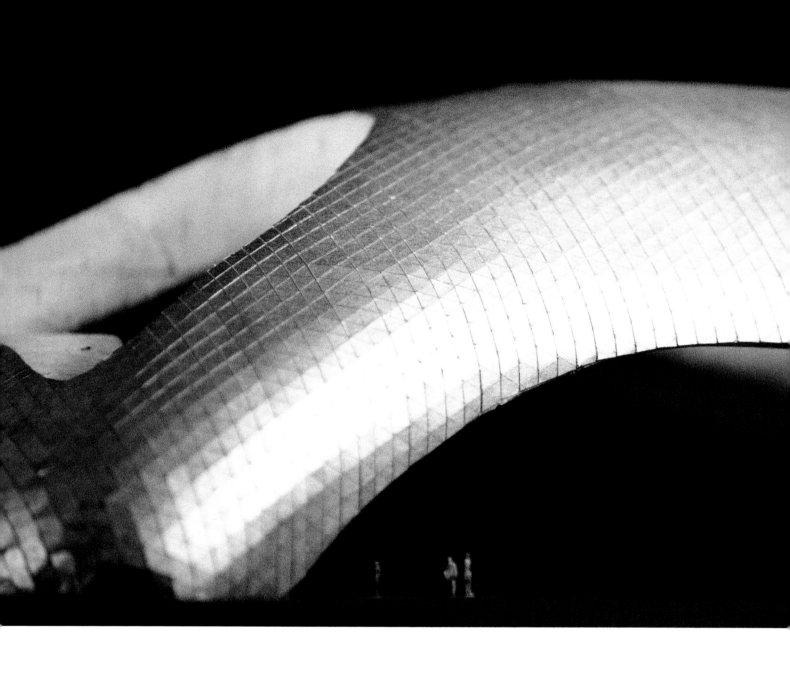

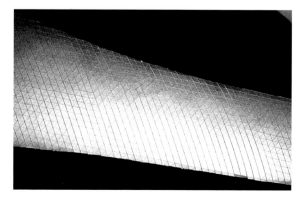
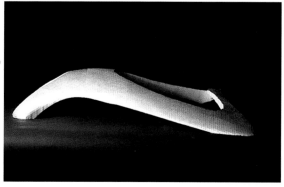

Integrated Transportation Centre, Seoul

One of the largest construction projects in the world, the Inchon International Airport in Seoul will form the gateway to what is hoped to be a reunified Korea. It will cater for 60 million passengers per year.

The project is being developed on reclaimed land, 45 minutes due west of Seoul. At its heart is the Integrated Transportation Centre, designed by Terry Farrell & Partners in association with Samoo and DMJM. The nodal point for the transport access system, it includes four railway links, below-ground car parking space for 5000 vehicles and a people-mover system.

The client's requirement for a grand gateway to the airport has been met by the dramatic design, which provides a sense of arrival and orientation while achieving new standards of operating efficiency.

The Great Hall exemplifies this with its 180m clear spans, reminiscent of the great Victorian railway stations, creating a magnificent window to the airport with views of arriving and departing aircraft.

The combination of the aesthetic with the functional is carried through to the below-ground car park, which provides the opportunity for creating a landscape garden setting at ground level around the Great Hall. A 200m triple-height pedestrian galleria linking the car park with the Great Hall provides a powerful aesthetic element in the landscape and acts as a fresh air supply plenum to the car park.

The scheme is currently on site and is due for completion in the year 2000.

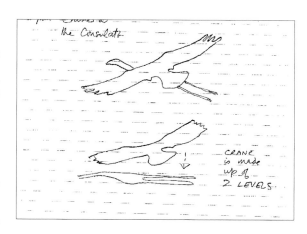

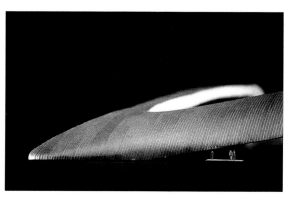

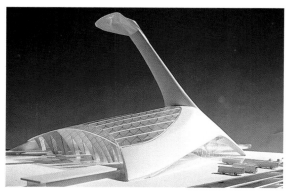

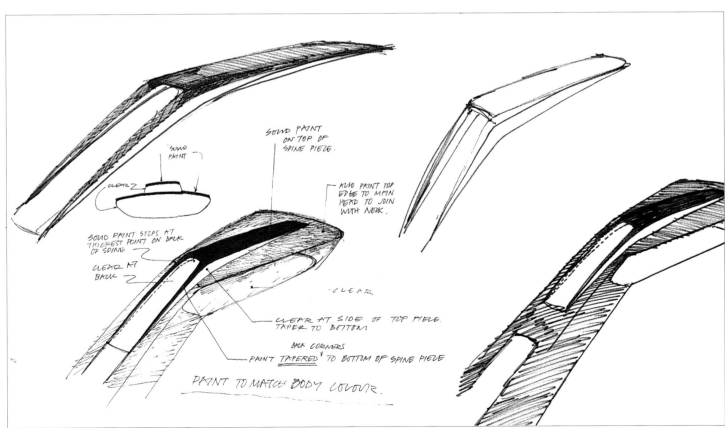

SOLID PAINT
ON TOP OF
SPINE PIECE.

SOLID
PAINT

CLEAR

ALSO PAINT TOP
EDGE TO MAIN
HEAD TO JOIN
WITH NECK.

SOLID PAINT STOPS AT
THICKEST POINT ON BACK
OF SPINE

CLEAR AT
BACK

CLEAR

CLEAR AT SIDE OF TOP PIECE.
TAPER TO BOTTOM

BACK CORNERS
PAINT TAPERED TO BOTTOM OF SPINE PIECE

PAINT TO MATCH BODY COLOUR.

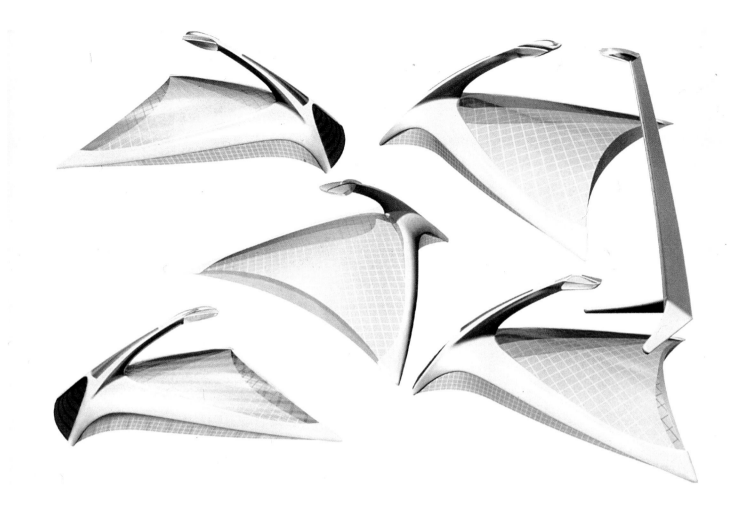

The extremely complex three-dimensional nature of the Great Hall roof proved difficult to capture in drawings and so its form was developed through a series of hand-carved models. Having settled on the approved silhouette, the selected model was sliced into many sections. These were then digitised to provide a series of CAD sections which were meshed together to form a three-dimensional computer model that accurately represented the original. From the CAD model, it was possible to produce an infinite number of accurate plans and sections which could be used to form the basis of the detail design package. In addition, the three-dimensional mesh was linked to a CNC (computer numerically controlled) machine which cut scaled 3D models that were then used for presentation and design development, including wind tunnel testing.

This process has been extremely effective as both a design tool and as a method for translating sketch models into production information.

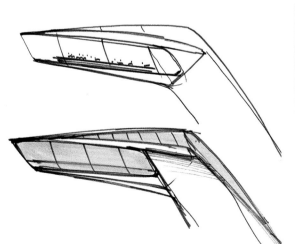

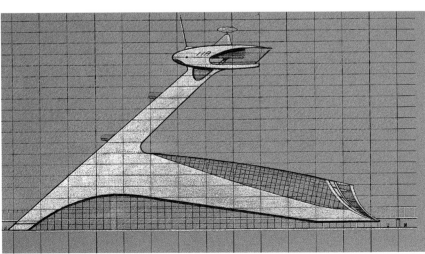

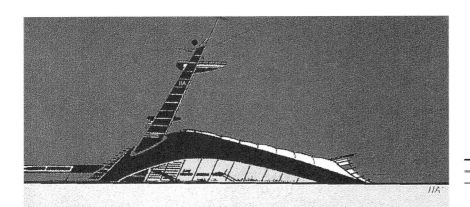

The key functional element of the Great Hall has been developed into a sculptural icon for the entire airport development which reflects Korean culture, nature, flight and the future. The organic-shape roof is clad in stainless steel panels on a steel superstructure and is capped by a 35 x 15m glass aerofoil which acts as a wind tower, harnessing the prevailing winds. This draws air via the gardens, which function as natural air filters, into the concourse area, thereby providing natural conditioning of the space for approximately half the year. For the rest of the year a tempered climate is provided in a 3m zone above the floor, thereby avoiding the unnecessary expense of air conditioning the whole volume of the Great Hall.

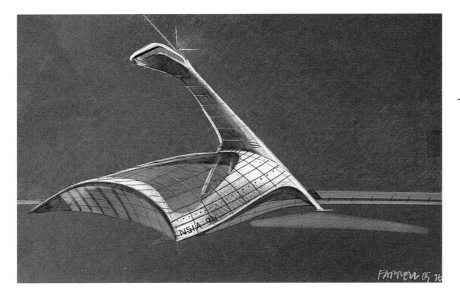

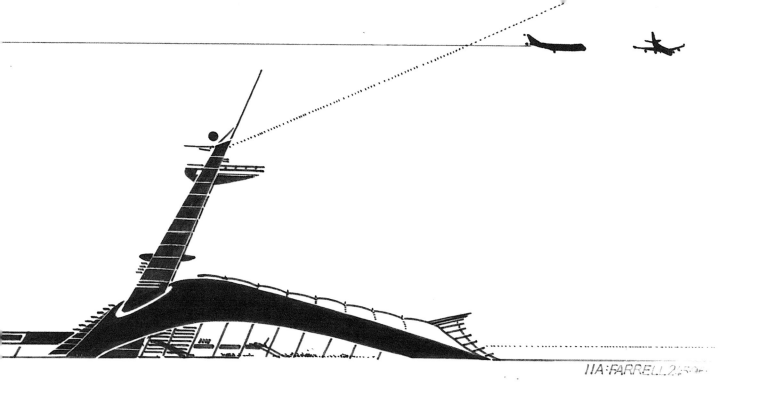

IIA·FARRELL 2·5·9?

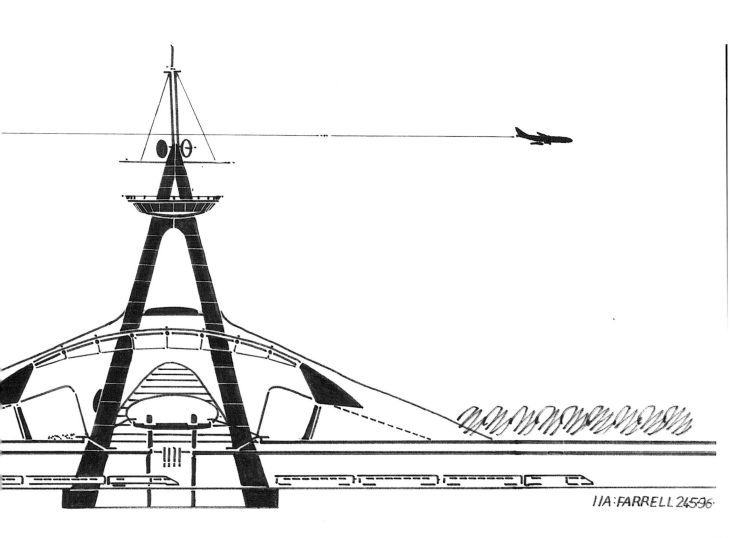

IIA·FARRELL 24596

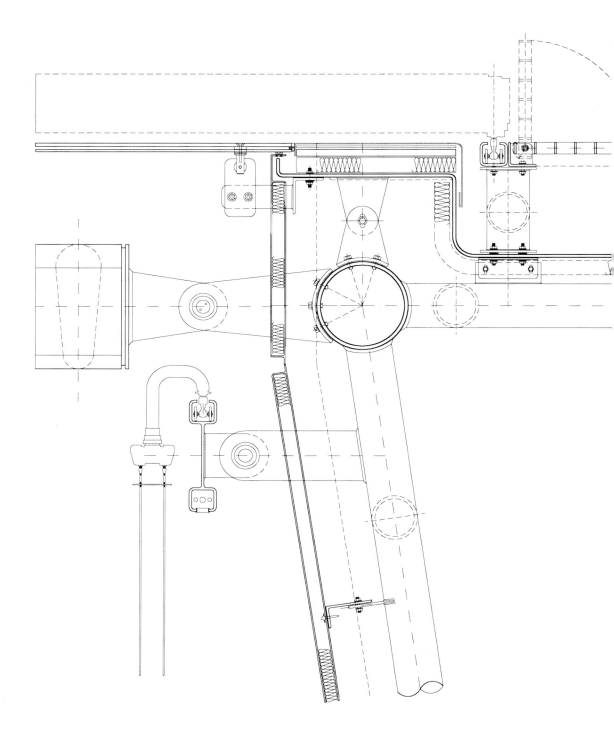

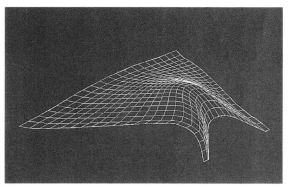

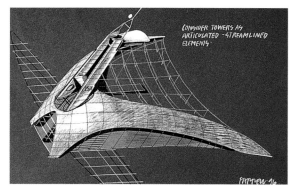

CONSIDER TOWERS AS
ARTICULATED -STREAMLINED
ELEMENTS-

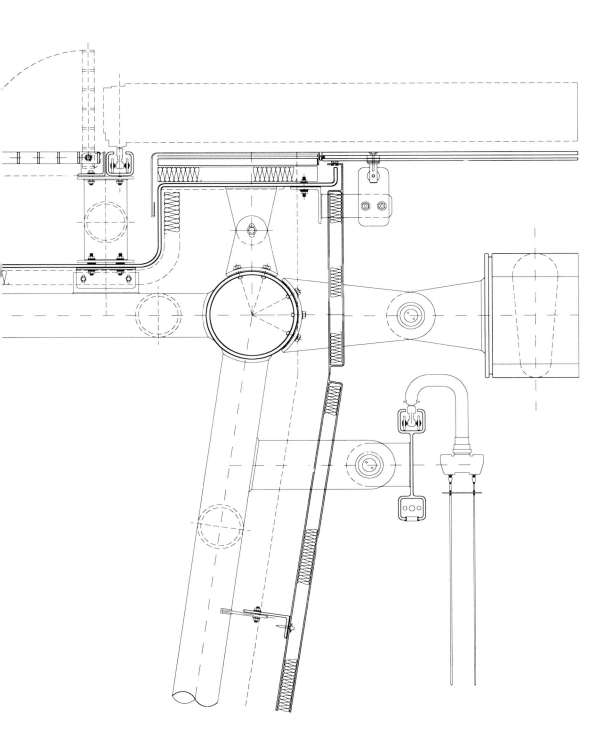

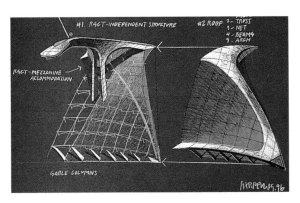

#1. RGCT-INDEPENDENT STRUCTURE   #2 ROOF   2 - TRUSS
3 - NET
4 - BEAMS
5 - ARCH

RGCT-MEZZANINE
ACCOMMODATION

GABLE COLUMNS

FARREN·09.96

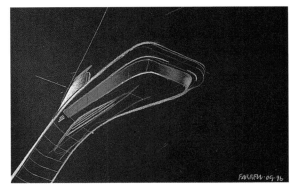

FARREN·09.96

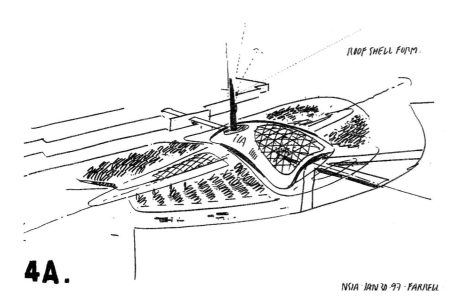

4A.

ROOF SHELL FORM.

NSIA · JAN 30 · 97 · FARREL

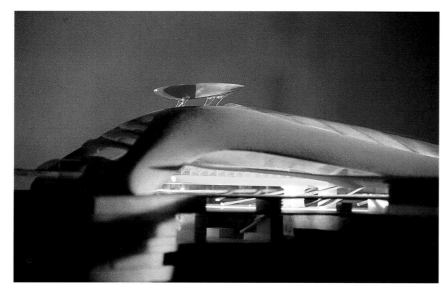

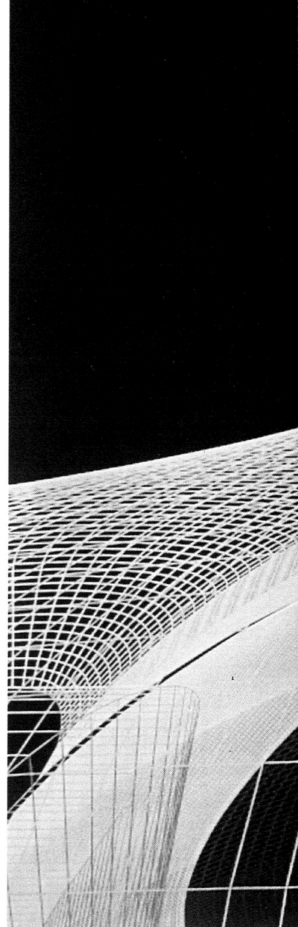

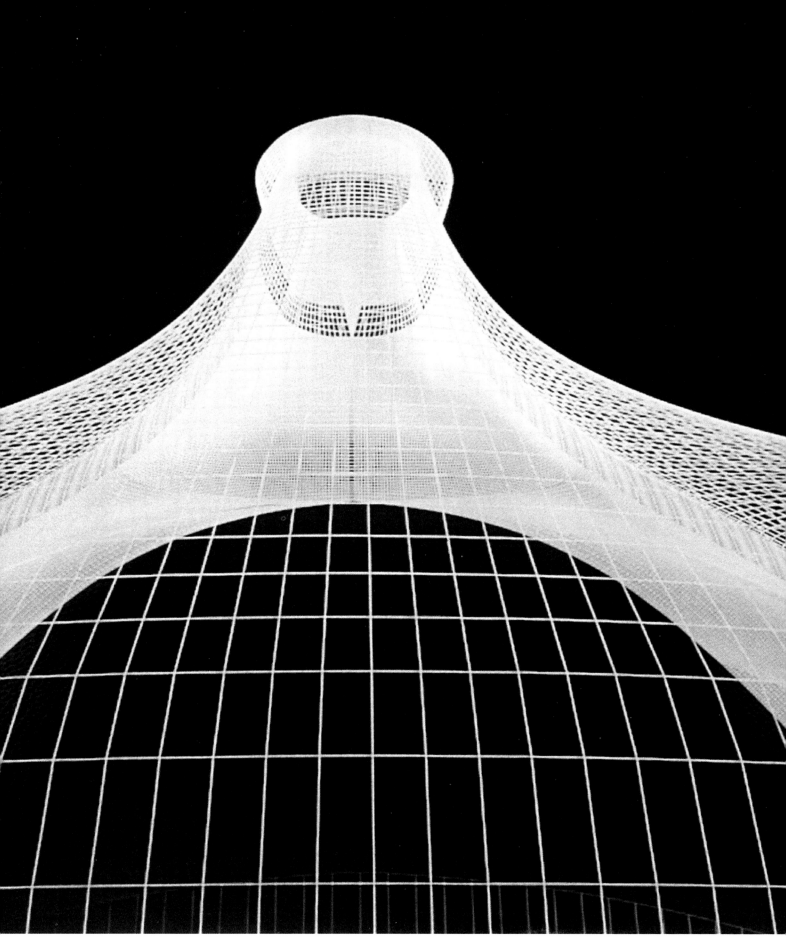

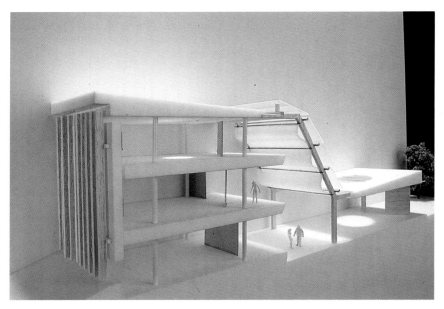

Computer Laboratory, Cambridge

Cambridge University Computer Laboratories Department, currently housed in cramped and fragmented city centre premises, is to move to new premises on a campus west of the city, adjacent to the M11 motorway. The masterplan includes plots for university departments, recreational and residential buildings. Terry Farrell & Partners was one of five practices invited to present their design approach.

The project focusses on flexibility of use, sustainability and engendering a community atmosphere. A 12 metre deep office space with circulation to one side was proposed. This gives access to a variety of room sizes and allows for future changes without disrupting the circulation. Service functions – kitchens, lifts and stairs, storage and computer rooms – are located in the middle of the plan, and the full width is used for larger laboratories. The main entrance and core are located centrally and secondary cores have direct access from the car parks to minimise travel to individual research units.

The north-south orientation maximises solar gains in the glazed south-facing spaces for winter and mid-season, while

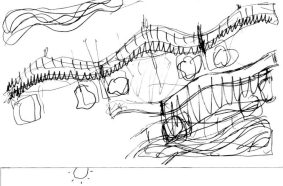

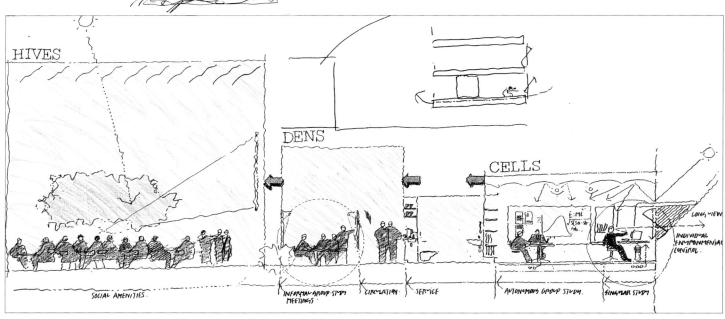

HIVES

DENS

CELLS

SOCIAL AMENITIES.

INFORMAL GROUP STUDY MEETINGS

CIRCULATION

SERVICE

AUTONOMOUS GROUP STUDY.

SINGULAR STUDY

LONG VIEW

INDIVIDUAL ENVIRONMENTAL CONTROL

allowing the north side to be highly insulated and make use of internal heat gains. The 12 metre plan depth allows for natural ventilation, and this is enhanced by the stack effect from venting the top of the 'street' glazing. The unheated, glazed 'street' acts as a buffer zone reducing heat losses.

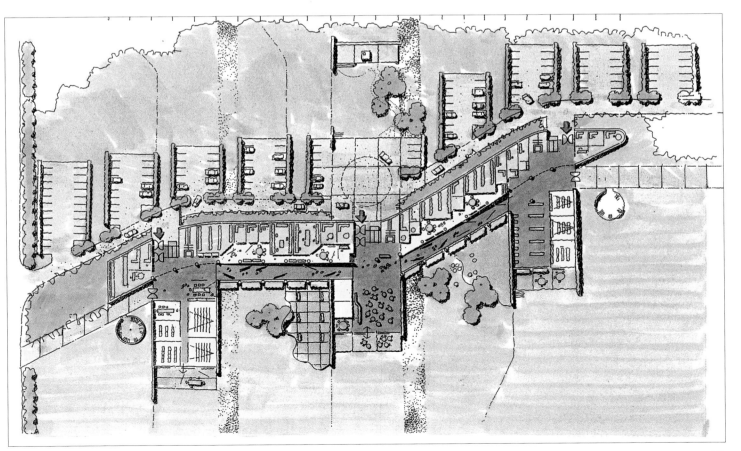

Maritime Square, Singapore

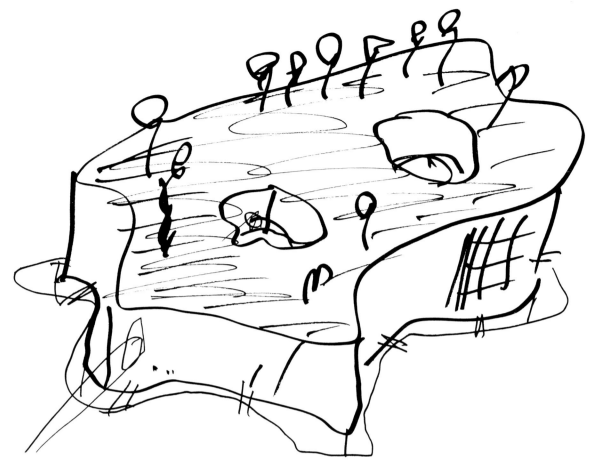

The brief for the phase one development of Maritime Square called for a signature waterfront scheme providing a mix of activities to attract local and international visitors – an icon for Singapore's aspirations. The concept is of an island in the plan shape of Singapore, surrounded by water – literally and metaphorically interweaving with the identity of the nation. The roof comprises a tropical park with trees, rivers and lakes, giving back to the citizens the land area occupied by the building. The undulating facade of transparent and translucent materials acts as a showcase for the activities within by day and night. A volcano-like office tower rises above the

roofline, providing a surface for projected images, and acts as a beacon viewed from the harbour and downtown. Central to the concept is the theme of water – starting as a spring at roof level, spilling into a lake, cascading as a waterfall into the central atrium down to a large internal lagoon where activities take place. In turn the lagoon feeds a river which meanders through the public spaces, eventually spilling over the podium edge into the 'sea' that surrounds the building.

Most of the drawings in this book are by:

Terry Farrell
Doug Streeter – design partner
Aidan Potter – design director
Steve Brown – design director
Bobby Desai – associate
Nic Sampson – associate
Eiffel Wong
Yutaka Yano

In-house CAD material:
Roger Simmons
Paul Treacy

Models by associate Chris Barber and his in-house team.

The following staff also worked on the featured projects:

Dominique Andrew
Emily Armer
Mohamed Azar
Susie Baker
John Barber
Chuck Barguirdji
Michael Barry
Dorothy Batchelor
Paul Bell
Rick Berman
Duncan Berntsen
Anthony Berridge
David Beynon
Nick Birchall
Andy Bow
Ingo Braun
Derek Brentnall
Toby Bridge
Angela Brown
Tony Burley
Collette Burns
Gary Butcher
Brian Calderwood
John Campbell
Darren Cartlidge
Brian Chantler
Grace Choi
George Clarke
Richard Cohen
Andrew Culpeck
Tony Davey
Susan Dawson
David Dawson
Bertil De Kleyne
Neil De Prez
Toby Denham
Philip Dennis
John Donnelly
Martin Earle
Kate Edwards
Gavin Erasmus
Martin Evans
Jo Farrell
Max Farrell
Sue Farrell
Grace Ford
Steve Fox
Adrian Friend
Sharon Galvin
David Gausden
Tom Gent
Maria Hadjinicolaou
Kelvin Hamilton
Thomas Hamilton
Jo Harrop
Sylvain Hartenburg
Wendy Hayward
Mark Hemel
Pyeong Heun Youn
Nicola Hibbert
Michael Hickey
Jim Holland
Nigel Horrell
Wayne Hosford
Catherine Hull
Maggie Jones
Tryfon Kalyvides
Sally Kendon
Tom Kimbell
Stefan Krummeck

Alexis Lammie
Mark Lecchini
John Letherland
Ian Livingstone
David Loughlin
Anya Louw
Kei Lu Chong
Euan MacKellar
Melody Mason
Peter McGurk
Ronnie McLellan
Brian Meeke
Tracey Meller
Annette Miles
Samantha Moffat
Giles Moore
Janice Morrison
Lorraine Mulraney
Donal Murphy
Paola Murphy
Ian Nickels
Derek Nolan
Anthony O'Brien
Ike Ogbue
Aye Otu-eyo
Louise Parker
Stuart Parkes
Dermot Patterson
Alexander Peaker
Louise Potter
Carol Riley
Jenny Roberts
Drummond Robson
Rajinder Rooprai
Michela Ruffatti
Shaun Russell
Arezoo Sadain
Martin Sagar
Mark Shirburne-Davies
Steve Smith
Philip Smithies
Alexandra Steven
Mike Stowell
Simon Sturgis
Paul Summerlin
Nick Swannell
Yoshi Takenami
Richard Tan
Catriona Thompson
Tim Thompson
Julian Tollast
Mimi Tse
Eugene Uys
Kees Van Der Sande
Chris Wakes
Tim Warner
Duncan Whatmore
Nick Willars
Tricia Williams
Simon Wing
Wolfgang Woerner
Chris Wood
Nicole Woodman
Jes Worre
Christopher Yee
Karin Yiannakou
Michael Young
Gary Young
Nigel Young

Valuable contributions were made by Sir Eduardo Paolozzi to the Dean Centre, Edinburgh, and by Charles Jencks with the landform sculpture for the Scottish Gallery of Modern Art.

Finally credit is due to the many consultants, external modelmakers and suppliers. A number of 3D CAD works were prepared by Virtual Artworks (Samsung Building, London). Most of the photographs are by Andrew Putler.